'Life consists of a series of events. Some appear to be pre-ordained and some are unpredictable. A lot of things can be put down to destiny or 'happenstance'... A curiously simple, yet complex twist of fate...prompted [the authors] to seek out some of the most fundamental human questions; questions about the meaning of existence and its ultimate demise, about the nature of love, in all its presentations and disguises...and ultimately, what can be gained (if anything) through 'loss'. In...*Love and Grief*, [the authors] boldly step into a labyrinth of spiritual and emotional paradoxes, guiding us alongside [some] intensely personal journeys.'

– Annie Lennox, solo singer songwriter

'What is it like when a partner dies? How can you cope after such a bereavement? *Love and Grief* is a book that is long overdue – it tackles the topic with compassion and insight and will be helpful both to bereaved partners and those who support them.'

– Susan Quilliam, relationship psychologist and agony aunt

'An honest and compassionate guide to the complex issues surrounding love after loss. It includes courageous personal accounts which offer insight into the often taboo subject of forming new intimate relationships following bereavement, and will be of great comfort.'

– Jackie Spreckley, Cruse Bereavement Care counsellor

'I feel this book fills an important gap in the literature of bereavement. Looking bravely at the often taboo topic of intimacy after bereavement, the authors capture the confusion of enjoying a new relationship while still feeling grief and even guilt. As this book draws on a wide variety of personal experiences, I believe that it will be of great value to the many who find themselves in this situation. They will realise they are not alone.'

– Denise Brady, St Christopher's Hospice

D1502707

of related interest

Relative Grief
Parents and children, sisters and brothers, husbands, wives
and partners, grandparents and grandchildren talk about
their experience of death and grieving
Clare Jenkins and Judy Merry
Foreword by Dorothy Rowe
ISBN 1 84310 257 9

Standing On His Own Two Feet
A Diary of Dying
Sue Grant
Foreword by David Clark
ISBN 1 84310 368 0

Without You – Children and Young People Growing Up
with Loss and its Effects
Tamar Granot
ISBN 1 84310 297 8

A Safe Place for Caleb
An Interactive Book for Kids, Teens, and Adults with Issues
of Attachment, Grief and Loss, or Early Trauma
Kathleen A. Chara and Paul J. Chara, Jr.
Illustrations by J.M. Berns
ISBN 1 84310 799 6

Children Also Grieve
Talking about Death and Healing
Linda Goldman
ISBN 1 84310 808 9

Someone Very Important Has Just Died
Immediate Help for People Caring for Children of All Ages
at the Time of a Close Bereavement
Mary Turner
Illustrated by Elaine Bailey
ISBN 1 84310 295 1

Love and Grief

The Dilemma of Facing Love After Death

Catherine O'Neill and Lisa Keane

Foreword by the WAY Foundation

NEW HANOVER COUNTY
PUBLIC LIBRARY
201 CHESTNUT STREET
WILMINGTON, NC 28401

Jessica Kingsley Publishers
London and Philadelphia

First published in 2005
by Jessica Kingsley Publishers
116 Pentonville Road
London N1 9JB, UK
and
400 Market Street, Suite 400
Philadelphia, PA 19106, USA

www.jkp.com

Copyright © Catherine O'Neill and Lisa Keane 2005
Foreword copyright © the WAY Foundation 2005

'Dead Woman' from *The Captain's Verses* (1994) by Pablo Neruda
reproduced with permission from Anvil Press Poetry.
Extracts from *The Prophet* (1997) by Kahlil Gibran
reproduced with permission from Wordsworth Editions.
'Into the Hour' from *New Collected Poems* (2002) by Elizabeth Jennings
reproduced with permission from Carcanet Press.

All rights reserved. No part of this publication may be reproduced in any material form
(including photocopying or storing it in any medium by electronic means
and whether or not transiently or incidentally to some other use of this publication)
without the written permission of the copyright owner except in accordance with the provisions
of the Copyright, Designs and Patents Act 1988 or under the terms of a licence issued by the
Copyright Licensing Agency Ltd, 90 Tottenham Court Road, London, England W1T 4LP.
Applications for the copyright owner's written permission to reproduce any part of this
publication should be addressed to the publisher.
Warning: The doing of an unauthorised act in relation to a copyright work may result in both a
civil claim for damages and criminal prosecution.

The right of Catherine O'Neill and Lisa Keane to be identified as authors of this work has been
asserted by them in accordance with the Copyright, Designs and Patents Act 1988.

Library of Congress Cataloging in Publication Data
A CIP catalog record for this book is available from the Library of Congress

British Library Cataloguing in Publication Data
A CIP catalogue record for this book is available from the British Library

ISBN-13: 978 1 84310 346 2
ISBN-10: 1 84310 346 X

Printed and Bound in Great Britain by
Athenaeum Press, Gateshead, Tyne and Wear

Zoe, Oliver, Luke, Nina, Emma and Peter,
we would like to dedicate this book to you as a way
of showing love and appreciation
for all you have gone through

Acknowledgements

We are indebted to all those people who gave us their stories so openly and honestly. We appreciate their bravery in sharing such private feelings to help others.

We would like to thank The WAY Foundation, which has been so helpful. This wonderful organisation gives much-needed support to people widowed before the age of fifty.

Our gratitude goes to Denise Brady in the Halley Stewart Library at St Christopher's Hospice for providing so much background research material and for giving us the confidence to pursue this subject. Thank you again.

Many thanks to all those who kept us going with their enthusiasm and food, including Oliver, who helped us with his invaluable computer skills.

Love and thanks to Tom, Finn and John for being family.

Contents

Foreword by the WAY Foundation   9

Preface   11

1   Grief   15
    Poem: Dead Woman   *22*

2   Past, present and future: The threads that connect even in death   23
    Death is Nothing At All   *29*

3   Living in a triad: A triangle of confusion, love and loss   31
    Poem: The Tortured Mind of Grief and Love   *39*

4   Mars and Venus   43
    Poem: The Bed   *53*

5   Through the eyes of a child   55
    Children Speak Out   *64*

6   Judgement: The world comes in   67
    Poem: Into the Hour   *72*

7   People's stories   73

Epilogue   141

References and bibliography   145

Useful contacts   147

Subject index   151

Author index   157

Foreword

Losing your life partner young is the perhaps the biggest trauma that can befall us. All the plans, the hopes, the dreams you have together are gone. Anger and bitterness may follow – at yourself for all those unsaid things, at your lost partner for leaving you. And worse, there are people to worry about around you, and people who worry about you. Their interactions with you and your interactions with them – your children, your in-laws, your friends – can change too. Your whole world is quite literally turned upside down, and it is a scary place to find yourself in.

How do you make sense of it all? The whole attention is on you – your grief, your life, and the lack of hope you feel when it first happens. I have been there, and I have come out on the other side. We are all so desperate for someone to really understand, someone who has been there and can support us because they know what we are going through. You are surrounded by so many people when you are widowed, but you are very lonely nonetheless.

Finding love again after the severity of this loss is something far from anyone's thoughts when we first face the bereavement. But over time, we have the capacity to love again. We are very different people following bereavement – it changes who we are. And it is possible to find love again when the time is right for you. Remember though that everyone is different. There is no set time period for finding love again.

Feelings of guilt and betrayal are natural. We as humans always think through all the angles, both positive and negative, but these feelings should not be barriers to taking that second chance. We know, after all, how precious life is and how we must make the most of it and take our chances when they come along.

Finding love again does not in any shape or form mean you are 'over' your lost partner. You will continue to grieve, and your new love must accept this as part of who you are. It is tempting to make comparisons between your two lives – the one you have lost and the one you are embarking upon with someone new – but in many senses there is nothing to compare – this is not an 'either/or' situation.

These are the very issues you will grapple with faced with this situation of finding love again. It is bewildering, confusing, heart-wrenching, but it is also rewarding to find happiness again.

The help of people in the same situation – those who really understand what it's like – is invaluable. I have found that invaluable group of people in The Widowed and Young (WAY) Foundation, which provides support to young widows and widowers for their grief.

But the issue of finding love again is one for which there is very little support and advice. In fact, the very source of your support through the grief can be the most difficult group of people from whom to seek this support and advice. I know many people in my situation who have reached out for that helping hand or listening ear, only to find that there is nothing there to help them through the rollercoaster of finding love again after bereavement.

Love and Grief fills that clear gap. It relates the stories of others who have suffered grief and found happiness again from which you can find hope, advice and empathy. It offers insight from a variety of situations – everyone is different – and, most importantly, it offers it to you in a non-judgemental way. Only you know how you are feeling, and what you are going through. Even those who are widowed cannot know exactly how other widows or widowers are feeling at that moment in their lives. It is a book I would recommend to those who want to explore love again, or learn about whether they are ready to make that transition. I would also recommend it to the in-laws, parents, children and friends of widows and widowers so that they can get a better insight as to how it feels to travel on that rollercoaster.

Sharon Whitehead
The WAY Foundation

Preface

In 2000, my close friend Evie was suddenly diagnosed with cancer of the liver. The primary source of the cancer evaded every test, leaving medical staff shooting chemotherapy at random at an unknown target. She died within five months, leaving behind three young girls, five, seven and eleven years old, and a shocked and grief-ridden husband.

During the months of nursing Evie, I began to admire her husband's kindness and unconditional love. We all loved together. There was a haze of grief and passion: passion to live, passion to hate the doctors, passion to find a cure (conventional or complementary) grief at the hopelessness, grief at the incompleteness, and many more tangled feelings.

These tangled feelings seemed to be sprouting many branches. It became an uncomfortable realisation that the love was becoming attraction between my dear friend's husband and I. There was an unspoken knowledge in the air.

Evie died at home with us. We lit candles, we played music, she spoke, although disjointedly at times. She did not want to leave this world at that time. She had no choice and we looked on in horror as she was eaten alive.

Her death reminded me of birth. It was a ceremony of transition. In my grief, I kept mistakenly calling the Macmillan nurse a midwife. There was some beauty in this pain. The blur of the funeral and memorial passed, and then the feelings amplified.

Christopher and I soothed our souls with our bodies. It was as if we were driven by some force, preordained – or is this a way of justifying our seemingly inappropriate, almost indecent, behaviour? We would make love and then cry into the pillow for her loss.

In the past, I remember pondering how on earth people managed to fall pregnant when they had lost a child. How could they do it, I wondered? Now I understand the therapeutic nature of physical contact.

Initially, the passion, the sex, the general confusion wiped away self-consciousness. However, as the former settled, the self-questioning started for me. Was he with me in mind or just body? He really belonged to his wife. I was, after all, in second place. I was plagued with memories of them kissing. I had sat at the hospital bed while they lay there cradled together like spoons. I had felt privileged to be there, but now this began to negate my self-worth within this relationship. It had its funny sides too. I was chatting at a party, expressing how difficult it was to have a relationship with your best friend's husband. The room fell silent as many shocked faces turned my way. Perhaps it would have been more decent to have added the adjective 'deceased' with 'best friend'.

I searched bookshops, libraries, the Internet to find accounts of others in my situation. There are a few paragraphs here and there, but nothing to bring empathy and justification. I began to find that the whole subject of love after death was somehow taboo. How, in this day of self-help books galore, can this be? I spoke to bereavement counsellors, the Natural Death Centre, the librarian at St Christopher's Hospice, which has an extraordinary range of books on death and bereavement. Nothing was available to help. My work as a speech and language therapist has taken me into the areas of grief and counselling. While working with people with neurological disorders, particularly those of a progressive nature, I have counselled people through their traumatic periods of change and loss. However, it has to be said that no matter how much clinical experience I had previously, nothing could have prepared me for the horror of seeing my friend die, or for the confusion of forming a relationship with someone who is grieving.

Having realised the confusion caused by grief and love merging, I felt that an empathetic exploration and sharing of experiences would be very helpful. There seemed to be a need to write a book on this seemingly taboo subject. I did not want it to be autobiographical, as this is so personal and private. However, I felt I had to be brave enough to step forward, using my therapy background and personal experience to ask questions. I asked my friend and colleague Lisa Keane to join me in collecting thoughts and different people's perspectives. We hope this will lead to an understanding of the process of love after death.

Finally, note that throughout this book we use the terms 'widow' and 'widower' when referring both to people who have lost a spouse and to those who have lost a long-term non-married partner.

Catherine O'Neill and Lisa Keane

Chapter 1

Grief

Grief, and all it brings, causes the emotions to swing back and forth like a pendulum, creating quiet desolation and inner chaos. There are strangely ecstatic moments followed, within seconds, by the sledgehammer of despair. The longing, aching, physical frustration of grief is second to none. It is an intensely personal experience. It may feel as if you are tuned into a different frequency from the rest of the world. There are days when you may be so detached that you are oblivious to whether you are wearing clothes, let alone whether the colours or the socks match. Your words seem to leave your mouth unselected, unfiltered. There is a feeling of there being a film between you and the world. Are you even perceiving things accurately? Are others behaving strangely, or is it you? There are minutes, turning to hours, when the floor becomes the magnet of your attention. It is quite indescribable and very solitary.

There must be a purpose to this physical and emotional response to loss. Emotional tears contain the enzymes leucine and prolactin. These are present only in emotional tears, not in the tears shed when peeling onions. They have a practical function in that they help the body to alleviate stress and cleanse itself of toxins. Crying itself is necessary, otherwise the emotions will build up and burst out in another way. 'Sorrow that has no vent in tears makes other organs weep' (anon).

Grief takes us to our core. It is not unique to humans. Animals can be heard howling when they experience the death of one of their own. Grieving is an instinctive primitive reaction. We have rationalised many other aspects of our behaviour, but still we have not rationalised our response to death. Perhaps this is because death is usually not a frequent enough occurrence over the course of a life to lead to the development of any rational responses. However, people have developed techniques to suppress their instinctive reaction. This can disturb the process of grieving, a process that needs to be gone through.

For a long time, we accepted Sigmund Freud's theories about what was happening to people when they were grieving. Freud thought that when someone was bereaved, they were trying to hold on to the lost person and include them in the structure of their present life. After a while, they would begin to realise that this was impossible, and they would refocus their energy into a new life and new relationships. He believed that once this happened, the person left behind would detach themselves from the old relationship and move on. It was over.

This is the opposite of present thinking. Now there is a movement towards the idea of 'continuing bonds'. The main essence of this theory is that the relationship with a loved one does not end with their death. A relationship continues between the grieving person and their lost partner. As they begin to move forward into new life and relationships, they are still connected to the old. This way of looking at things accepts this attachment as a positive factor that actually helps the process of moving on to new life. As with all theories, ideas will be evolving constantly as people try to understand such enormous emotions.

The cycle of grief

Elisabeth Kübler-Ross, a leading writer on death and grief, was the first person to recognise that the grieving process has a cycle. In her book *On Death and Dying* (1997), Kübler-Ross states that everyone goes through the same stages when they know they are going to die. When witnessing a death and when grieving a death, the same stages are gone through:

- Shock and denial
- Rage and anger

- Grief and pain
- Bargaining
- Depression, withdrawal into oneself and separation from others
- Peace and acceptance.

When a person is dying and is in the process of losing their life, they start with denial, which is a normal defence mechanism to cope with bad news. The anger phase sets in when they realise: 'Why me? Why do I have to die?' Rage can be focused in many directions, towards doctors, family or God. Then bargaining starts: 'Let me see our daughter's next birthday.' Depression is often experienced and is brought on by the person retreating into their illness and sleeping. This has been called 'the final rest before the long journey'. Finally, there is acceptance. Kübler-Ross feels this is more than resignation, which is what occurs when tears and anger are not shed. Acceptance brings peace.

These stages are mirrored by those close to the person who is dying. After the death, it starts all over again. It is common to see denial, shock and anger following a death. The anger stage sets in after the realisation that denial is no longer feasible, because death is final. They ask questions, such as 'Why my wife? Why not someone else's?' The bargaining starts when the bereaved person continues a kind of conversation with the person who has died. Depression and separation from others are very much to be expected in grief. Could this isolation be necessary to prepare for a new life? It may take a while to accept the loss of the old life before the new life can be embraced.

Recognising grief

Several decades ago, when someone close died, there was a tradition of wearing a black armband. This was helpful because it was an outward statement of mourning, showing that the griever was somehow in a different world from everybody else. It signalled to others to go carefully and allowed for empathy and care. When the mourner removed the armband, it signified they were ready to move on and were open to the possibility of a new relationship.

Western culture nowadays has very little structured mourning beyond funerals and memorials. If no religion is involved, then there are even fewer ways of marking the importance of what has just happened and very little guidance. School assemblies are one of the last places where there is some form of public ceremony acknowledging that something major has happened in children's lives. This kind of recognition can be extremely helpful.

It is intriguing that those cultures that have clear shared rituals about grief and mourning have an almost complete absence of prolonged grief. An interesting study compared Scottish and Swazi widows; it showed that although the Swazi widows displayed more initial tearfulness and distress, they were less troubled by feelings of guilt a year later compared with the Scottish widows. The explanation for this discrepancy was that the Swazi have clearly defined rituals for mourning. These involve public crying and saying farewell during a given period of time.

The parts played by culture and religions

Many traditional cultures have retained a sense that they need to express grief outwardly and symbolically to enable them to move on. In Papua New Guinea, people used to mourn close relatives with very specific rituals to make their loss and grief visible. A widow would stay inside her house for several months and make a bodice and cap from coix seeds. These seeds were significant since they were also known as 'Job's tears'. When the widow emerged, she wore the bodice and cap and plastered her face and shaven head with white clay, which puckered and scraped the flesh painfully as it dried. All the deceased person's female relatives also plastered themselves with the clay. After wearing the bodice and cap for a year, the widow symbolically removed them and threw them away. Then she could remarry.

Many other symbolic rituals in traditional cultures recognise the fact that when someone dies, there is still a connection to them. This connection with the spirit world is very present in everyday life. Religion also talks about this continuing relationship. However, there is a whole realm of attitudes to what this means within different religions. There is a world of difference between an Irish Catholic approach and a Protestant approach to the dead and dying, even though they are both Christian and both believe in an afterlife. Irish Catholics anoint their dying and hold wakes for the dead. The more reserved Protestants surround death with quiet murmurs and respectfulness. The more scientific Western assumption is that the death of the body equals the death of the self. This contrasts strongly with the Eastern view that death is just a transitory incident of ongoing existence. Michael Dunn, in his excellent *The Good Grief Guide*, notices that rituals performed in other cultures are much more established. These lengthy and elaborate rituals note the upheaval in family relationships. They are outward acknowledgements of the changes that death has brought.

Christianity

Although Christianity has lost many of its rituals over time, some rituals still remain within more traditional cultures. Some Greek Orthodox widows dress in black for the rest of their lives. This is because it is believed that death is not final or separating but only temporary until the woman is together again with her husband in Heaven. This is an affirmation of the continuing relationship. After the funeral, there are ongoing rituals consisting of services spaced out at increasing intervals: weekly, monthly, then three-monthly for twelve months, and then yearly after that. This process is called *Mnemossina*. It is expected to be officiated for ever because of the never-ending relationship with the deceased. This ritual reminds others of the grief that people are experiencing, which does not go away just because the funeral is over. Outsiders can forget quickly. Although Greek Orthodox widows remain dressed in black, Greek Orthodox widowers are not bound outwardly to their wives for so long, and it is expected that they will remarry.

Judaism

Judaism has strong rituals following a death. These rituals have evolved to give respect to the dead, to comfort the living and to channel grief. There are specific actions that need to take place both before and after a person dies. The family of the dead person 'sit *Shiva*', in which they stay in their house for seven days while friends come to pay their condolences.

Candles are burned day and night, and mirrors are covered. No new clothes are bought for a whole year. Grievers do not join in with any entertainments or celebratory events for a whole year, an observance called *Avelut*. After a year, the mourning period is over and further grief is discouraged, except for a yearly anniversary service, *Yahrzeit*. There is a more Orthodox Jewish ritual, called *Halitzah*, that releases a childless widow from the obligation of marrying her brother-in-law. One of the original aims of this ritual was to give her a child in her husband's name (see Rachel's story in Chapter 7, page 85).

Islam

The Muslim view is that death is very much a part of life. A bereaved Muslim will feel a strong sense that God wants them to live and move on. Muslims are buried facing Mecca. On the third, seventh and fourteenth days after death, prayers are said in the mosque. Mourning should last no longer than three days, after which everyone is encouraged to 'return to normal'. The exception is a woman mourning her husband, who will be expected to mourn him for four months and four days. After that, no one should talk about the dead person. New relationships are accepted in the Muslim tradition because life and death are accepted as natural processes and beyond our control (see Fatma's story in Chapter 7, page 109).

Buddhism

The central belief of Buddhism is non-attachment. This means that there is a less sharp sense of loss and bereavement following a death. It is important that the body is allowed a period of peace for the spirit to move on. Six weeks later, Buddhists believe that the spirit attaches itself to an embryo to begin a new life. Mourning lasts for a hundred days, during which time relatives will be supported by friends and monks. Due to the importance of letting go, there is an emphasis on wishing the dead well in their future life through prayer. This lack of attachment allows the widowed person to continue in this life without referring to the past.

Hinduism

Hindus have strict rituals following a death. The body is cremated on the same day and the funeral pyre lit by the deceased person's eldest son. There is singing and wailing while people wait to hear the skull cracking in the flames to show that the spirit has finally been released. The ashes are then scattered in flowing water. The widow will wipe away her wedding mark and will wear a white sari for the next year. There are further rituals at one, three and six months. Widows should not remarry for a year, but widowers are allowed to marry far sooner. Some Hindu societies consider remarriage an unforgivable sin. Although it is now illegal, some ultra-strict Brahmins still practise *sati*, in which the widow throws herself on the funeral pyre. This practice came about because a wife was seen as a possession of her husband and, consequently, her life was regarded over when his was. In some communities, the widow is expected to stay 'frozen' where she was when her husband died: that is to say, she cannot further her education or improve herself but is expected to spend the rest of her life doing menial chores. She loses all her property and possessions.

'Pardon me, but I shall go on living'

In the initial period after losing a partner, while feeling the desire not to live on, many people may want to commit 'emotional *sati*' and feel frozen at that point in time. With this preoccupation with the past, it seems impossible even to contemplate a new life and relationships. Dilemmas surface. Is it alright to enjoy life without feeling a sense of betrayal to what has gone before? There may be guilt for not having loved enough or not having shown it enough. After his wife committed suicide, a widower said:

> When Marina died, I actually knew what true love was – when it was no longer available to give or to receive. And the hollow of that experience has grown steadily and heavily as the initial shock that carved it out of me has wearily eroded.

Anger and guilt at things left undone can also torment. Emotions are not static, and many conflicting feelings can be present at the same time. It *is* possible to feel desperate at your loss *and* to enjoy a film or time with friends. Sometimes, people feel they should wear a shroud of gloom, even to the point where they feel guilty when they shed it. No matter what, the past will always be there. Life and relationships that come after loss will be affected by it.

When grieving, we are learning about living as well as about death. We learn about ourselves from how we react. It can be an experience of growth, even though it is at a price of great pain. We have to face ourselves, now, in the present, living without the person dearest to us. It is important to surface into life. The stories in the second half of this book will show how people can go forward into the future. 'Grief is a tree that has tears for its fruit' (Philomen *c.*300 BC).

Dead Woman
Pardon me
If suddenly you do not exist
If suddenly you no longer live

I shall live on.

I do not dare
I do not dare to write it

For where you have no voice,
There shall be my voice.

No, forgive me
If you, beloved, my love

If you
Have died,
All the leaves will fall on my breast,
It will rain on my soul night and day
The snow will burn my heart,
I shall walk with frost and fire and death and snow
My feet will want to walk to where you are sleeping

But I shall go on living.

(Neruda 1994)

Chapter 2

Past, present and future

The threads that connect even in death

What is eternity? When you fall in love, what you want most deeply is to be together for ever. No one ever enters into a meaningful relationship expecting it not to be eternal. In wedding vows, we say the words 'Till death us do part', not really believing in death, let alone an early death. Somehow we imagine magically dying together. Most literature talks about love being for eternity or the hope that love will last for ever.

This feeling increases as two people grow more interdependent over time. Is it just because life is easier when you are together, or is it the blending of life and soul over the years? Many people report how they have observed their parents go through various stages in their relationship and emerge closer in old age. A sixty-year-old widower speaks of his wife's death as like losing his best friend:

> I would be at the window if she went out; I couldn't wait until she came back. To see her coming down that hill and pull up in the driveway after an absence was almost orgasmic. That's how it was. She felt the same way about me.

Queen Victoria continued her devotion for her husband for more than four decades after his death, even needing to solidify her devotion by building memorials.

What is this attachment between two people about?

In a study looking at the remarriage of widowers, Moss and Moss (1980) talk about the five recognisable aspects of any relationship. These aspects are about all the different types of interaction that give a feeling of continuity between two people and bind them together. They make both people feel secure and protected. The five aspects they defined are:

- Caring
- Intimacy
- Family feeling
- Commitment
- Reciprocal identity support.

Caring grows out of years of affection and mutual concern for the welfare of each other.

Intimacy grows out of daily interaction. Those small insignificant details that make up a life together help people to anticipate the perceptions and reactions of each other. Partners often develop a pattern of communication and interaction unique to them. This sets them apart from others and solidifies their sense of bondedness. Sex and physical contact are obviously also fundamental to intimacy.

Family feeling is the way in which each person becomes involved in, and part of, the other's family system.

Commitment is established through behaviour, thoughts or words. It is shown in the promises made between two people that demonstrate they intend to maintain their bond with each other. This is also furthered by planning life together.

Reciprocal identity support refers to how being part of a relationship affirms your own sense of self and identity. Each person is moulded and formed by the other as the partnership develops over the years.

Once a partner dies, what happens to all that closeness?

Can these attachments be undone? Is it healthy to do so? What happens to these five aspects of attachment when one partner dies? Does holding on to any of these aspects actually help a person to move on? The mourner will reconstruct their life in a way that allows these attachments to continue, but in a different form.

After a partner has died, the survivor will go on *caring* for them, hoping that they are happy, wherever they might be. They may have a sense that the dead person is caring for them by watching over them with concern and care. Widowed people will often want to carry on the legacy of the person who has died and complete their unfinished business where possible.

A feeling of *intimacy* is continued as they wonder what the dead person would have done or thought. The bereaved may even have internal conversations with them.

Family feeling continues because each member of that family will have had a unique relationship with the person who has died. This reinforces the family system and keeps the feeling of a joined family alive. The house that the couple lived in and the objects they chose together carry on this aspect of attachment.

The widowed person maintains a *commitment* to their dead partner through thoughts and actions. There is a sense of loyalty to the person who has died.

The widowed person continues to do things that they know the other person liked or valued. This is one of the ways that *reciprocal identity support* continues. It is common to see widows who have never remarried continue the role of the wife into old age. Some widowed people almost take on the identity of the other person.

Moving on to a new relationship

When a widowed person moves on to a new relationship, the five attachments involved in any close relationship have to be adapted to include the
new person. The old attachments will certainly have a strong effect on the
new relationship. There are complicated connections taking place. The
dead partner travels into the new relationship in the memory of the
widowed person. Through this memory, the dead person exists in the
present for both people in the new relationship. The memory of the
person will always be there, therefore, as the new relationship develops; it
will continue into the future. The new person will be involved directly in
the way these attachments evolve.

Caring for the dead partner persists, although maybe in more subtle
ways. A widowed person may worry that feelings of affection for a new
person will diminish their caring for their first partner. They will need to
develop ways for the two kinds of caring to coexist. The widowed person
will often reassure themselves that their dead partner would be happy for
them to be happy, even with someone new. Is this because they feel that
their dead partner would care for them enough to wish them happiness?
This feeling of continued caring allows them to move forward without
guilt. Family occasions and other important events all bring back
memories and are occasions when the widowed person feels the tie most
strongly. These feelings resurrect the previous relationship. The new
person in the relationship will find themselves involved in this process.
Most cultures recognise that these occasions are very significant times
and will have rituals to mark them.

Intimacy with the dead person still exists, even when a new relationship has started. Even if a conscious effort is made not to talk about the
first partner, unexpected memories will be triggered and intrude in
everyday life. Memories of the dead person are evoked in all areas of
domestic life – music, cooking, shared events. Claire, the new partner of a
widower (see Claire's story in Chapter 7, page 76), tells how even in a
most intimate moment in bed, she felt the presence of her husband's dead
wife. The widowed person may sometimes mistakenly use their first partner's name. However, the fact that someone has shown the capacity in
their previous relationship to be intimate can be very positive for future
relationships. They may have learnt successful ways of living with

someone else, which can be drawn upon in a second relationship. One woman bravely commented that a widower was attractive as he had already been 'trained'!

A widowed person may feel that they cannot express their feelings about intimacies in their past relationship as it might be too difficult for the new partner to hear. This means they may develop a strategy of protective silence. They may feel it appropriate to put away photographs but keep other things that evoke the past that the new partner might not be aware of. A remarried widow told how she put away most things from her life with the dead husband but left other things around the house without her new husband realising their significance. She was trying to protect him and reduce any possible insecurity.

Family feeling is rearranged by a new relationship. Other members of the family become involved when outward signs of the new relationship, such as living together or remarriage, start to occur. This creates a new framework for all three families involved, which, of course, includes the dead person's family. Each of the new partners enters the new relationship with his or her own sense of family. This sense will remain but will also be blended into the new. Family members can feel displaced and may need to find a new position in the family framework. A parent whose daughter has died may fear for her position as a grandparent when her son-in-law remarries. Will she be at all relevant in their new lives? Elsie, after her daughter Anna died, felt excluded by her son-in-law's new partner. She felt his new partner found the situation difficult:

> I feel that Maria has difficulty with me because I was part of Anna. My relationship with my grandson is an extension of Anna's existence and this seems to be threatening to her.

Restructuring the family is a very delicate area, particularly for children, who will have loyalties to their dead parent and may worry about betrayal. Unlike in a divorce, these children have seen their parents continue to love each other. As their parents' love was arrested by death, rather than a life decision, they may wonder how their surviving parent could possibly love another.

However, children will be one of the main reasons why there will still be a connection with the dead person's family. Children embody a lifelong tie with the dead parent. This will come up in all kinds of ways, in appearance, mannerisms and behaviour. If the new partner is the one who helps the children celebrate their dead parent's anniversaries, then they will be involved inextricably in their continued affection and attachment. This brings the new partner into a direct relationship with the dead parent. Sarah (see Sarah's story in Chapter 7, page 126), the new partner of a widower with children, told how it is *her* role to celebrate anniversaries and to take the children to their mother's grave.

Commitment continues because the widowed person feels they should try to hold on to the past. This can lead to feelings of guilt once a new relationship starts. They may feel that they do not think of their dead partner enough. Simon (see Simon's story in Chapter 7, page 80) expresses a sense of unease when he realises he has not thought of his dead wife for a long time. He deals with this feeling by splitting his thoughts into compartments. He describes how he feels that his first wife is still around, but 'just in another room' (see 'Death is Nothing At All' at the end of this chapter). He feels he can go and visit that room whenever he wants. However, he says that he does not go there as much now, as life goes on.

Where there is such a strong attachment between two people, how is it possible for anyone new to enter this situation without being an intruder? There can be a romantic attraction towards a widow or widower, but their attachments to the past can make the situation very complicated. Conflicting emotions bound around for all the different people involved. The new person can be tested to the limit by feelings of jealousy and insecurity.

Starting a relationship with someone who is *recently* widowed is almost taboo. There are certainly difficulties. The widowed person is wrestling with the confusion of new-found love while trying to find ways of continuing to love their dead partner; the new person is trying to find a place to fit into an established loving attachment. Friends and family often have not moved on from the death as fast as the widowed person and may not understand. Simon tells how he felt that his new relationship had propelled him forward in his grieving process, while his children were left behind in theirs.

The sense of self that people give each other in a relationship, *reciprocal identity support*, is the aspect that shifts most when a bereaved person starts a new relationship. It has to change to include the new partner. However, it is difficult to purge from our history those who have been close to us without damaging ourselves mentally. It is not necessary to delete them completely, but it is important to be open to forming a new identity with a new partner. This shift does gradually take place. In the second relationship, it is impossible for the identity of the bereaved person to remain static as each day they have new experiences and grow. Although the widowed person may tend to see their identity through the first relationship for quite some time, the new relationship may start to give them new insights into their personality. This can be particularly marked if the first couple got together when they were young. They have grown up in relation to their partner. Tim, a widower, described how in his first relationship he had been dependent. In his new relationship, he was discovering more self-confidence. Mahmud (see Mahmud's story in Chapter 7, page 92) says:

> I am not the same person I was when my wife was here. I have been changed by the bereavement. I suspect you change even more in time.

The previous sense of self will persist, however, alongside the new. The experience surrounding the death of a loved one will obviously affect a person's self-esteem. Self-esteem is a constantly moving barometer of our inner self and will be affected by the past, the present and the future.

How does a widowed person create the space in which two loves can exist at the same time? People often refer to visualising their lost partner in a different room in their mind 'somewhere very near, just around the corner' (see 'Death is Nothing At All', below). This allows them to have two loves side by side. A bereaved person will need to find their own way of living with the past in the present, while moving into the future.

Death is Nothing At All
Death is nothing at all. I have only slipped away into the next room. I am I and you are you. Whatever we were to each other,

that we are still. Call me by my old familiar name, speak of me in the easy way which you always used. Put no difference into your tone; wear no forced air of solemnity or sorrow. Laugh as we always laughed at the little jokes we enjoyed together. Play, smile, think of me, pray for me. Let my name be ever the household word that it always was. Let it be spoken without an effort, without the ghost of a shadow on it. Life means all that it ever meant. It is the same as it ever was; there is absolutely unbroken continuity. What is this death but a negligible accident? I am but waiting for you, for an interval, somewhere very near, just around the corner. All is well.

(Henry Scott Holland, cited in Emerson 2004)

Chapter 3

Living in a triad

A triangle of confusion, love and loss

Most religions claim that when someone has ceased to be in a physical sense, there will be an eternal relationship with them in the spiritual sense. Despite this, they normally see marriage as 'till death us do part' and allow the remaining partner to move on. Mormons, however, are unique in believing that a marriage is for eternity: 'When a marriage is performed by the proper authority, in the Holy Temple, it can last through eternity' (www.mormon.org). They feel that this promise gives a sense of eternal commitment.

Even though most people do not believe that marriage or long-term relationships are eternal, they accept that there is a continuing relationship with the person who has died. Once a widowed person forms a new relationship, however, there will be three people involved in the relationship. Being part of this triangle can be confusing and can have an effect for a long time, even to the end of their days. In the first relationship, the couple may have planned to be buried together. Where does the new person fit into this plan? The previous plan has to be re-evaluated. This highlights the difficulty of the situation.

The solution to this sensitive situation will evolve naturally with time if handled sensitively. Both Kerri and Mahmud (see Kerri and Mahmud's stories in Chapter 7, pages 88–98) commented how strange it felt to realise that, all being well, they would eventually be together longer than they had been with their previous spouses. Mahmud said he found this realisation scary, not because you are entering a relationship with someone else but because 'You fear that it somehow diminishes all that passion and emotion that you had in the first relationship'.

Loving two people: the widowed person's perspective

The person at the apex of the triangle is the widowed person. This is the person who maintains a tie with the past at the same time as building a tie with the present. It requires a great deal of strength and empathy on their part to balance this. Feelings of betrayal and guilt do enter along with the excitement of a new love. If new love happens soon after the death of their first partner, then it comes at a time when they are grieving and perhaps feeling fragile and confused anyway. This situation of being in the middle may not always have been quite so difficult and uncomfortable. There is a seventeenth century painting, on view in Tate Britain, which graphically depicts this three-way relationship. The dead and the living intermingle easily together in this picture of a widower shown looking admiringly at his living wife while also holding the hand of his dead wife. This image would be more emotionally shocking if it was depicted so literally today.

Esther (see Esther's story in Chapter 7, page 133) remarks:

> In previous times, when life was short and people died more often at an early age, it was much more accepted that people married again. A man would need a woman to look after his children, a woman would need a man to support her, and so on. Life was very tough and people were more pragmatic, but now there is embarrassment. There is not the obvious necessity [for remarriage].

A widowed person may initially feel guilty about loving someone new, or they may fantasise about how wonderful their dead partner was, but, in time, these feelings become more realistic. Ironically, although there is a great deal of hurt and grief, it often seems as if the widowed person finds living in this triangle more straightforward than their new partner does.

What has happened has happened and the widowed person cannot afford to look back and wish for things to be different. This finality of death often makes them realise how short and precious life is. They may feel that they must embrace it because life is for living. Fatma (see Fatma's story in Chapter 7, page 109) says:

> I really do love my first husband and I still miss him. I do not feel bad about this. It is just a fact… I feel that I have accepted my new life.

One widow says she feels that it is much easier to lose someone through death rather than divorce because 'it is a divine act which you have to accept'. It is a divine act as opposed to the human act of divorce. Divorce can be harder to cope with because of the rejection of love.

Boxing with a phantom

The person who is most disadvantaged in the triangle is the new person coming in to the relationship. He or she must always 'box with a phantom'. Strangely, when questioned in academic research projects, only a minority of people confessed to any jealousy or resentment of the 'phantom'. However, in the stories in this book, the new partners have been very honest and universally confessed that being the incoming person can be emotionally threatening. Perhaps this reticence about confessing these real feelings stems from the fact that this is a very sensitive subject. Is this the taboo of not speaking ill of the dead?

Although the ideal is just to accept the existence of the 'phantom' in the new relationship, this is very difficult in real life. The new partner may in some way feel insecure, perceiving themselves to be a second choice. Society refers to the dead partner as the 'first', which has the connotation of 'better', 'chosen', 'preferred'. 'Second' suggests second-best. In many situations, a comparison is made between the two. Underlying fears about this can evoke feelings of insecurity, which means the person needs to have their worth and importance positively affirmed by their partner.

The experience of being the new person in this triangular relationship is depicted graphically in the novel *Rebecca* (1938) by Daphne Du Maurier. The heroine marries a widower. When she returns with him to live in his house, she feels the threat of Rebecca, his beautiful socialite dead wife, everywhere. The heroine very much finds herself in the role of second-best. When she is shown the room that the housekeeper has chosen for her, she says: 'I found myself installed in something inferior... a second rate room, as it were, for a second rate person.' Acquaintances make her feel second-rate when they say of Rebecca: 'Of course, she was so clever' and 'You are so different from Rebecca.' The housekeeper glorifies the memory of Rebecca and deliberately tries to undermine the heroine with comments about Rebecca's perfection and insists on following exactly the way in which Rebecca did things around the house.

It is interesting that the domestic details are the most eroding when the new person moves into the 'old' house. Many people describe the cooker as being an area of the house where they feel the presence of the dead person. People who knew them say how strange it is to see a new person standing there. Elsie, whose son-in-law remarried after the death of her daughter, tells the new partner: 'I am sorry if I seem diffident with you, but it is very difficult for me to see you here in the kitchen where my daughter was.' The dead person's presence is all over the house. The heroine in *Rebecca* describes feeling haunted by how '...there were things which Rebecca had touched. Perhaps in cupboards, there were clothes that she had worn with her scent about them still.' She also refers to finding around the house 'the little notes, the letters, page after page, intimate, *their* news'. Similarly, one new partner also describes these signs of little intimacies being thrust in her face, forcing her to acknowledge her partner's previous unended love. She minds, she says, because she would prefer to believe these intimacies were unique to the new relationship.

There can be a feeling of being in someone else's place. This can feel awkward in situations like sitting in *his* place at dinner parties or in the front seat of the car where *she* used to sit. If the new partner knew the dead partner, then they will have actually seen the original couple together, and this can exacerbate the feeling. It takes a while for these internal pictures to be changed.

As the new person adjusts to the situation, they will find ways to change the environment around them, allowing them to feel comfortable. They try to create a world around them that is unique to this new relationship. They may paint the house a new colour, dispose of the old marital bed, or quietly move away photographs of the dead person. As their confidence grows, they may assert their individuality more and more. This helps both partners to make the adjustment needed to form their new identity as a separate couple. Claire (see Claire's story in Chapter 7, page 76) tells how one friend gave her very good advice when she pointed out that her husband's dead wife had never been interested in the garden. This meant that this was something she could make her own, and it is very important to her that she has managed to do this. It is as though she has been able to mark out her own territory.

All this can seem very harsh to onlookers as they see aspects of the first person being removed or changed. It appears as though they are being eliminated. But, for the new relationship to develop, the new person has to take their space. This should not be confused with replacing the memory of the dead person. Grieving outsiders can react strongly because they have not grieved at the same rate as the immediate griever. They need these outward manifestations as symbols of contact with the person they have lost.

Glorification

No one wants to speak ill of the dead. In fact, in death, most people become larger than life. 'He was a giant of a man', 'She was an angel.' Kerri talks of a fellow widow's relief when she expressed something negative about her first husband:

> [She felt] most people made out that their late partner was the bee's knees. Ian was not perfect; far from it, and neither am I. He was a wonderful man and I loved him.

I suppose when you are grieving, you do remember the good times and what you have lost. For the widowed person, this glorification is just an expression of their love, but for the new person, it is this glorification that can be one of the biggest threats. They may feel this threat even when the widowed person is outwardly trying to be realistic about the human frailties of their dead partner. The imagination can run riot as to ways in which the dead person could have been better than them. This can lead to feelings of inadequacy.

This glorification of the dead is the thing that most undermines the heroine's new relationship in *Rebecca*. She hears people say: 'I believe she was very lovely. Exquisitely turned out, and brilliant in every way. They used to give tremendous parties at Manderley… I believe he adored her.' This description makes the shadowy phantom in her mind become even more real.

Dying young means remaining eternally young, and this is a fact that a new partner has to live with as they themselves age on a daily basis. How can you compete with a beauty that never grows older? Rebecca has 'a beauty that endured and a smile that is not forgotten…'

The feelings of inadequacy can be amplified when the new partner has known the dead partner. It is hard when the dead person's qualities have actually been seen and their goodness cannot be denied. Esther talks about marrying her dead friend's husband: 'I had rather a lot to live up to. She was my good friend, she was a wonderful woman, a wonderful cook – it made me feel inadequate.' Claire, who knew her husband's dead partner, talks about '…the perfect family. They had these three beautiful children and they were the centre of the village social scene.' When his wife died, she talks of 'a perfect picture cracked in half'.

Accepting the existence of the phantom

In order to move on, it is important to come to terms with these natural feelings of insecurity and threat. Acceptance is the key, but *what* you accept and *how* you get to the point of acceptance is an intensely personal journey. Research shows that the chances of a new relationship working are more favourable if the new partner can accept the widowed person's tie with the dead partner. It is important that they come to terms with the fact that, were it not for death, the old relationship would have continued. It was not broken voluntarily as in a divorce. Claire acknowledges that although it bugs her that her husband still wears his wedding ring from the previous marriage: 'He did, however, have a whole life with her and you can't suddenly say "Sorry, it's me now".' She has learnt to accept the dead partner's place in their relationship, although she finds it difficult at times.

To help the new partner accept the situation, the widowed person can adapt their daily life and social interactions to accommodate them. It is important that they recognise the fragility of the new person's position. Simon (see Simon's story in Chapter 7, page 80), a widower talking about his new partner, says:

> I think the person who has had the hardest job has been Claire. *She* is the person that needs congratulating. It is a very difficult situation coming in on a bereaved family.

The new partner may feel like an intruder. They are entering an emotional field that has deep roots in the past and need to be helped to feel welcome and valued. For this to happen, it helps if the widowed person learns to be aware of the deep fears that their new partner may feel. It also helps if they actively try to give them confidence in the validity of the new relationship.

Could there even be a need for overcompensation? When Simon recognises how hard it must be for Claire, it makes her feel good about herself. She feels as though she is in her rightful place and not a usurper. However, if a widowed person acknowledges qualities in their new partner that their first partner might not have had, then it can feel like a betrayal. A bereavement counsellor says it is important *not* to feel guilty and to have the confidence to affirm both these similarities and differences. To counteract any danger of the new partner feeling compared, they need plenty of reassurance, both honest and open. Differences and similarities are not to be feared, otherwise feelings of insecurity can fester inside and grow out of proportion.

These honest comments are needed to help the new partner feel validated. They need it more than someone who has come from a broken relationship not involving death. As time passes, this reassurance will not be required so much, as both people in the new relationship grow and change. The widowed person will be moving away from the deceased, and the new partner will be established more firmly in their new world. This all reduces the sense of being an outsider. Acceptance by the family is crucial. When Claire, the new partner of a widower, met her mother-in-law-to-be, she felt valued when her partner's mother said: 'She will do very nicely. She is like a breath of fresh air.' Claire said: 'This gave me the confidence to walk in on what everyone viewed as a perfect family.'

If both people are widowed, then it is less likely that they will be 'boxing with a phantom'. They will have been through the same experiences. They can accept what has happened: they will not feel so threatened by each other's yearning for their lost loves. It creates a balance as they both have another love.

The dead partner's perspective

So often, widowed people talk about what their dead partner would have felt about their new relationship. This somehow allows a glimpse of the dead person's perspective. Their voice is heard in inner conversations. There is often a sense that they would be very happy for their surviving partner to have found happiness with someone else. Kerri, after she had grieved a while, says: 'My husband would feel I had done my time… He would be happy as long as who I chose is good to the children.' Sarah (see Sarah's story in Chapter 7, page 126), who married her best friend's husband, also feels her friend would be happy and relieved that her children had found a new mother. She even feels that her friend would be pleased that 'they were enjoying each other'.

If there is guilt in the new relationship, then the inner conversation will become more negative with the dead person. People may perceive that their dead partner is upset or angry. This may be due to insecurity about the present, and perhaps in this case bereavement counselling may help. This feeling is rare, however. In all the research that we undertook for this book, most of the widowed people we spoke to felt their dead partner looked on their new relationship with happiness. Mahmud asks himself how his wife would feel if she were in his position, having found someone so soon after she had died. He says:

> The human part of me says I would be upset, but there is no going back. I would want her to be content and you cannot have it both ways.

Many people report how the dead partner actually feels present. They even feel their presence in intimate moments. Kerri actually thought she saw her dead husband in her new partner's face as they were making love. She felt as though '…he was giving me his blessing and saying "It's fine".'

'Heaven'

There is the thorny issue of all three people in the triangle meeting up in 'the next life'. Which partner would the widowed person be with? Simon, a widower, says he cannot imagine the three of them in Heaven. Claire, his new wife, laughingly rejected the idea, saying: 'Oh no! She will be still young and beautiful whereas I will be old.' Rachel (see Rachel's story in Chapter 7, page 85) relates how her second husband used to joke and ask which husband she would choose to be with in Heaven. She just said: 'Ah, that would be telling.' Fatma was also asked the question by her second husband. She laughed and, as a Muslim, she answered with the story of the Prophet and His nine wives. The Prophet answered this question by saying: 'It is up to the wives to decide.'

Kerri, a widow who is now with a widower, says:

> I am not sure I believe in God any more. I suppose it is because I am angry… But Mahmud and I have laughed about what would happen if there was a Heaven. Would it be all four of us together? Would we all swap stories? We both said that, if one of us goes, at least we know that there will be someone there to meet us.

The Tortured Mind of Grief and Love
It is a schizophrenic existence
I split my mind in different directions and feelings to accommodate
What am I juggling in my mind?
A lost dear friend I grieve for
Versus a woman who has left
Much work left undone and much to do
I swap from one thought to another

Oh, my dear, dear friend
Where have you gone?

I now sleep with your husband
We share the experience of his body

I startle at the realisation of your death
Yet I feel happy to be with your husband

If you had not died where would I be?
If you had not passed on,
Would you have stayed eternal lovers?

You and he were very close
How could I possibly mean anything after that intensity of love?
Who will he be with in the next life?

You were tall and slender? His type. I am not
He married you for your legs. I hope it is a joke. What about mine?

I remember you lying together cradled like spoons
I feel like a fork

I remember your laughter together,
My mind erases your arguments
It tortures me

My thoughts jump back and forth
I see my new found love

I turn my head a fraction and see 'you' together
I turn again to the present and struggle with love and guilt

I want to love you
To remember you
And, oh, how I want to eliminate you from our new love
How, at times, I want to criticise you
To pull you to pieces
To make me feel stronger, better, the best
A need for superlatives becomes an obsession

Your eternal youth and beauty frozen in time and the mind's eye
I age daily, even faster now I am picking up the pieces
The debris from before and after your death

You have the ethereal advantage
You can be glorified
I am the reality
No fantasy shrouds me

Am I competing with an angel or a ghost?

I cannot win
Just stop, do not torture yourself – you may say

I cannot yet

Time conquers all
Is it beyond my control?

I seem to have grown many heads
Each reacting with a different emotion to this love triangle
Thoughts are processed rapidly and jump from one head to the
    other
At times the heads are so heavy, I feel crushed
At other times I feel giddy with love and lightness

Does he think of her when we love?
How can he not?
He says not
I would
I do
Does he not have feelings?
Are his emotions so different from mine?

At times, I feel second place
I have spent many years knowing you together
When I meet old friends and family
It feels as if I am wearing the wrong skin

It should be you, not me
You and I were close
We laughed together and confided in each other
I curse our intimate gossip of your marital bed
It plagues me now
Now I do not want this precious and amusing sharing
I felt honoured at the time
Now it erodes the present

You said you wanted this
You hoped for me for your children
Did he choose me?
Did he fall into this through need and physical desire – men's
    stuff?

Perhaps it was beyond our control
Perhaps it was preordained

Rationalisation for the cynical
Faith for the believers

I have to accept your love
I have to know that our love will grow
Yours will remain but ours will magnify
I have to step forward
I have to fill this space in your world
I have to love and be loved

All will be well
With time

Chapter 4

Mars and Venus

Coming together after a bereavement has many implications for both people involved. The widowed person will have to deal with many new experiences before they feel comfortable being with someone new. In the relationship that has just been cut short, they will have moved with their partner through various phases, during which they learnt about each other, eventually settling into the quiet dependability of being a couple. Now energy will be needed to move in the reverse direction. Skills that have been redundant now have to be resurrected in order to start a new relationship. Doing this may feel embarrassing and awkward. Will they ever be swept off their feet again as they were when they met their first love? This is all so difficult because they are still in love with their dead partner. Ideally, they need to feel they are an authentic individual in their own right and not just a victim of loss.

Many questions may come up before they feel ready to start a new relationship:

- How can I repeat the unrepeatable?
- Have I the energy and commitment to give to someone else?
- Am I betraying my dead partner?
- Having struggled to learn to be alone, how do I give up my independence?

There are positive sides of new relationships second time around, however. You are older and wiser; you have learnt how to love; you know how valuable life is. It can be seen as a chance to have a new adventure, a new sexual relationship, something that you had not expected.

Sex

Physical intimacy is a basic human need, and after losing a partner there can be an aching sexual neediness. If their partner had a long illness before they died, a widowed person may have missed this sexual part of their life. Richard (see Richard's story in Chapter 7, page 100) talks about his experience before his wife died:

> Where cancer is involved and the partner has been very ill, operated on, pumped full of noxious chemicals and irradiated to look like a week spent on a beach without sun cream, then there is not much intimacy… [so] those left behind are keen for sex.

Sexual frustration will have built up. This can even lead to resentment and then guilt. After a person's partner dies, and while in an initial shocked state, they can be tempted to find comfort through brief sexual encounters. These may act as instant gratification and allow the displacement of real feelings, but they may also be useful as a release for pent-up emotion. However, they are unlikely to fill up the emptiness.

A widowed person who had sexual relationships before they entered into their long-term relationship is more likely to be motivated to seek a new partner than someone who has had only one relationship before. Kerri (see Kerri's story in Chapter 7, page 88) says: 'It was strange being physical with someone new. I had only ever had one partner…'

The idea of finding a new relationship can feel bewildering. Once it starts, fear of inadequacies of the physical side of things may arise. The widowed person will be used to their dead partner's likes and dislikes and may be uncertain of their ability to please someone new. There may be a preconception that romance equates with youthfulness, so they may be reluctant to expose their 'ageing' body. However, it seems that older people actually have greater skill and capacity than younger people for forming new loving, sexually fulfilling relationships. Do you remember the clumsiness and inexperience of youth? In fact, Claire (see Claire's story in Chapter 7, page 76), who married a widower, says that their new sexual relationship is much better than either of their previous relationships: 'As he and I are older, we are more experienced and therefore more relaxed in bed.' It seems as if age somehow allows people to take the initiative and discuss their sexual needs.

Widowed people may be surprised at how much better sex is with a new partner. Simon (see Simon's story in Chapter 7, page 80), a widower, says:

> Both of us feel very lucky to have been given a second chance. Second love is very different from the first. You have learnt things in one relationship which you can put into practice in the second.

However, this positive feeling can bring its own guilt and regrets. Tim (see Tim's story in Chapter 7, page 120), a widower who formed a new relationship with Sarah soon after his wife's death, describes how sex was very soothing to his grief. He confessed to Sarah that sex gave him a feeling of closeness that was physically and emotionally addictive. However, he found his feelings about it very complicated. Sarah herself (see Sarah's story in Chapter 7, page 126) tells how he would make love to her and, immediately after, would feel the need to say to her: 'I don't love you. I love my wife. This is just sex.'

Claire, who married a widower, admits that, occasionally in bed, she felt: 'This should not be me.' Her husband was much more pragmatic and took great pains to '…tell me that she and I were so different.' For some people, it can take a while before they are ready for this closeness.

Differences in grieving

It appears that there is a great difference in the ways in which men and women grieve. There is also a difference in their timescales for moving on. This is a factor that has arisen constantly in the interviews for this book. In gay relationships, these differences will not be defined so clearly and there will be other subtle patterns. More traditional cultures have recognised this difference by setting up separate traditions for men and women after bereavement. Most of these require women to mourn for longer than men. It is more common for women to exhibit their grief outwardly in the way in which they dress. This is not expected of men, who instead are often actively encouraged by those around them to replace their dead wife quickly. Although Western culture no longer uses such outward manifestations, there is still an implicit expectation for women to grieve for longer and to remain alone for longer. However, although it is widowers who date sooner initially, research shows that both widows and widowers will be dating equally frequently by the thirteenth month after a partner's death.

There are many other differences. Men can enter into romantic relationships with a wider age range of women. It is acceptable for older men to be with younger women, whereas the reverse is not so accepted. There is even a difference between how men and women perceive their ties with the dead partners once they start a new relationship. Neither is less tied, but these ties have different emphasis and meaning. With all these issues surrounding them, it seems inevitable that men and women will react in different ways.

Mars: the male perspective

When bereaved, it is men who seem to cope better at first. But two to four years later, it seems it is women who have recovered most. A sad statistic shows that there is a sixty-six-fold increase in suicide amongst widowers compared with a ten-fold increase for widows. Is this related to the way in which they have grieved? Is there something about the dynamic of the relationship between a man and a woman that explains this? In her book *Men and Grief* (1991), Carol Staudacher found that when most men discuss the loss of their partner, they reveal how the partner had three main roles in their life: domestic partner, sexual partner and companion. A man has often relied on the woman as a surrogate mother. Some men come to realise that there were many chores and responsibilities in the home that they were never aware of before. If they have young children, they will now be solely responsible for all the childrearing tasks. This may be something that they were involved with only partially before their partner died. Richard tells how, shortly after his wife died, he was in the swimming pool with his two young children:

...with one going one way and the other going the other way thinking 'What now? Which one do I go after?' ...nothing did prepare me for being left totally alone with two kids, even though I had been a modern father.

Even if previously he did share in childrearing tasks, a man may still be shocked by the myriad details to keep an eye on. He is now responsible not only for the children's emotional needs but also their schedules, appointments, homework, and so on.

Everybody needs physical closeness and tenderness when they are grieving, but men often feel they can experience this only through sex. They feel comforted. This same need for comfort may lead men into forming sexual attachments before the death of their partner, although this is an uncomfortable taboo. A man may suffer greatly over the loss of physical intimacy, perhaps more than a woman. When his partner dies, he may long for his partner's touch, her smell, her voice. Her clothes and her perfume may possibly offer sensory comfort. Although grieving, the sexual drive can still dominate his thoughts and actions. This drive is a strong component in men. They often wonder: 'Does being without my wife mean that I'll be without sex for the rest of my life?' 'How long should I wait before I'm with another woman?' They may want sex before they feel society would approve of them having it.

At the other end of the spectrum, there are men who fear impotency when they have lost their partner. It is as if this equates with losing the masculine side of themselves. Bob, a sixty-year-old widower, confesses:

I'm impotent at the moment. I hope it will go away... It would be terrible if it didn't. A man's virility is the one thing that satisfies his ego. If he were to lose his virility, then he may think 'What else is there to live for?'

While the fear is real, the probability of being impotent is not. It may occur quite suddenly through trauma, but usually it is not permanent and subsides as the grieving process moves on.

In his book *It Takes A Worried Man* (2002), Brendan Halpin talks with brutal honesty about these sexual feelings. When Brendan's wife was diagnosed with breast cancer, he decided he would write what was real to him about his experiences: 'Fear, lust, annoyance, love, fatigue, resentment, existential terror, horror movies, alcohol and country music.'

His wife jokes that, after she has died, he can have meaningless relationships but not remarry. He writes that he had already been musing
about this and admits to using sexual fantasies as a way of denying 'the
whole horrible nightmare'. He is uncomfortably aware that his wife's
illness and possible imminent death are transforming him into a tragic
figure for women and, therefore, a 'babe magnet'.

This sudden arousal of sexual feelings towards someone other than
one's partner can feel very surprising. Brendan confesses very honestly to
noticing 'how foxy his wife's oncologist was' and finds his hormones are
out of control. He looks at other women all the time, 'even more than
usual', and cannot help finding his wife's nurse attractive, because 'she
takes good care of us all.' This attraction to a carer is a common occurrence, and it is not unusual for a man to marry the dead partner's nurse.

It is common for widowers to feel that they have no idea who they are
without their partner: 'I have become Brendan Halpin, spouse of a cancer
patient.' This feeling will change as the man constructs a new separate
identity for himself. Widows may feel they have lost this sense of self, but
not so keenly.

Men may bury themselves in work or have affairs to avoid their
feelings of pain and loss. Brendan says: 'I have thought and heard about
guys who have affairs during this time.' Although this displacement tech-
nique could be viewed as a mainly male trait, a female gay colleague of
Brendan's told him how, when her girlfriend had cancer, 'All she could
bear to do was to work or she would go insane.'

'Being alone is unbearable'

One widower reflected that his wife 'was the person who made the world
make sense'. In *The Hazard of Being Male* (1976), Herb Goldberg writes
that 'the male unconsciously comes to see the female as his lifeline, his
connection to survival and his energy source.' Many adult men, once they
have established a relationship with a woman, begin to abandon almost
all of their other relationships. Very often, therefore, his partner may have
become his only confidant and true friend in life. She may feel like his
defender, his foil between himself and the world, his main focus. This can
often equate with dependency. Mahmud (see Mahmud's story in Chapter
7, page 92) says that in his bereavement group, there is a lot of banter on
this subject:

> A lot of women think that men cannot cope on their own…men do not have close male friendships in which they can offload their feelings… they find they can only get this in a new relationship.

This could be due to the fact that men relate to men differently from the way in which women relate to women.

When a man's partner dies, because she may have been the one who provided their social life, he may lose his contact with the outside world. Unless he has an external structure, once he is on his own, he may turn to a more internal life involving thinking about the past, drinking and watching TV… His partner's death requires a man to face the world with no intermediary. Men may be angry with themselves when their partner's death reveals how needy and attached they were. There is a feeling of loss of power and a heartfelt cry of 'What am I supposed to do now?' Being alone can be unbearable.

It seems, statistically, that men are more likely than women to fall ill themselves following the death of a partner. This can be either physically or psychologically. All this seems to point to the possibility that men are better off than women being married.

Closing doors

Men seem to have a different emotional sensitivity from women. Simon talks about some of his behaviour after his wife's death, saying:

> I do not think blokes go through it in the same way. They do not think too much, really, particularly physically. They act before they think rather than think before they act.

He explains how it was his new partner who had to point out that they needed to replace his old marital bed. For him, it did not have the emotional resonance of connection with the past as it did for his new partner. Men react differently from women when they start new relationships and find different ways of protecting themselves from their raw feelings. One of the defence mechanisms that men use is sex, which takes them away from the present.

Once he begins a new relationship, a man will have a different perspective on the process of moving on. He will be far more able to cut off from the past and close doors. Richard, a widower, tells how in his bereavement group he just '…wanted to shoot the breeze and talk about a way forward, whereas the women wanted to go over and over what they had been through.' Because he was ready to move on so quickly, he tells of '…lots of false starts. Hopefully not too much damage done to others.'

Venus: the female perspective

Women are resilient and seem to cope alone better than men. The general life expectancy of widows is reduced by six months, whereas that of widowers is reduced by eighteen months. However, since women seem to grieve slower than men, it can take longer for them to be ready for a new relationship. Interestingly, research shows that only 43 per cent of widows ever have a sexual relationship after they lose their partner, as opposed to 82 per cent of women who are divorced (Dunn 2000). One of the contributory factors to this statistic is that women outlive men.

A childless widow will move on faster than a widow with children and seems to enter into a new relationship almost as quickly as a man. Anne (see Anne's story in Chapter 7, page 82) tells how the month after her husband died, she went to the hospital to ask the palliative care staff whether they knew of any dating agencies:

> I felt dreadful as it was so soon after but all my friends were in couples… I felt a lot of guilt. How could I lose Paul and want to try and move on so quickly?

Belinda (see Belinda's story in Chapter 7, page 105), childless at the time of her husband's death, tells how he had said to her: 'Give it six months to make it look decent, then go and find someone else.' She did not intend to follow his advice, but she soon found herself in a relationship with someone they had both known for some time.

A widow is often not 'sought out'. Perhaps this is because she does not exude as much need as a man. She may be taking more time to process her grief, and this is visible from the outside. If she does have children, then a man may not be naturally attracted to her as he may not want to take on another man's children. There could be a Darwinian factor involved where women are attracted to nurture the young while men seek to continue their own line. A widowed mother's overriding concern is the happiness of her children. This has been stressed over and over again in the interviews for this book. Marilyn (see Marilyn's story in Chapter 7, page 73), a widow who has not formed a new relationship, says:

> My children are everything to me. I have to hold back. They did not ask to be born and they are my responsibility. I am human and I am attracted at times to men. It is normal, I am a woman.

Fatma (see Fatma's story in Chapter 7, page 109) reiterates that her children are her priority. Speaking of her new partner, she says: 'I chose him because he is good to my children. A younger man might just want *me* and not my children. I am older now and love is different.' Even once these mothers are ready for new relationships, there is the difficulty of finding someone because they have their children in tow. Kerri, in answer to her family saying 'You need to get out and meet somebody', replied: 'How the hell am I going to meet someone pushing a pram around the park?'

A grieving woman is less likely than a grieving man to soothe herself with sex, particularly if she is older and has children. Due to the nature of female relationships, a woman is more likely than a man to receive comfort through her friends. She will be less likely to seek a sexual relationship as the only way of gaining physical and emotional tenderness. If she has children, then she may be less attractive to the opposite sex. A woman may see a widower as a 'little boy lost', whereas a man may see a widow as a tragic figure rather than a sexual being.

The 'little boy lost' brings out the nurturing instinct in women and they will be drawn in flocks to look after the 'magnetic' widower. Claire was at the funeral of Simon's wife: 'I saw Simon and I thought he looked so amazing. It was like he had an aura around him. He held his head up high.' Conversely, a widow may be seen as a threat. Perhaps this is due to the image of the 'merry widow' and its connotations that she is 'rich, free and ready for play'. Historically, this came about as many marriages were arranged for financial security; in some cases, a woman could have felt relieved to be free from her husband by his death. Widows often talk about being ignored and left out of social events. Esther, a widow (see Esther's story in Chapter 7, page 133), says:

> Women are often excluded socially because so many people play the numbers game… at dinner parties, people are prepared to make an extra place for a man whereas a spare woman will be regarded as a threat or a nuisance. A man alone will never have difficulty getting invitations.

When her partner is ill, a woman will be more steadfast, whereas some men may feel the need to back off and may start to fantasise about other relationships. Is this because women are nurturers and are tied into relationships in a different way? Elizabeth (see Elizabeth's story in Chapter 7, page 98), a psychotherapist, states: 'Men do not seem to form the depth of bond. Women are more bonded in any relationship than men.' This generalisation may or may not be resonant; obviously, many men do form deep bonds, but these may be different from the female type of bond.

There is a struggle between balancing grief and being in a new relationship. However painful, it is worth battling and progressing to the future. On a lighter note, research shows that there is an added perk, as a much higher percentage of widows than married women have orgasms each time they make love!

Coming together

When you start a new relationship, how you approach it will be shaped by your past. There will be many factors involved, including your experiences of previous relationships, the length of your relationship, the type of relationship you had with your partner, and your age at the time of their death. Most importantly, what will shape a new relationship is your ability to love, even if this feels that it has taken a bashing. You also carry your values with you, and you may revert to what you already know.

If you had many relationships before your long-term relationship, then you may find it easier to be out there again. However, Anne shared her fears: 'I don't know the rules any more.' She questions whether the world has changed but, not knowing, the only thing she can do is to draw on her past values and experience.

Letting the grief out, learning to understand yourself and redirecting energy into ideas, things and people all contribute to wellbeing. Moving on to a new relationship that involves all these things can be very healing.

To survive loss well, it is better to be open to the possibility of receiving affection and to respond to love when the time is right. Mars and Venus, although different planets, are essential to each other.

The Bed

We sat by your bed absorbing
The diagnosis
The end of life
It could not be

We lay in your bed remembering
Times, events together
Times of shared maternity clothes
Sharing worries about birth,
Children and love

We sat on your bed, choosing
Wigs to cover the ravages of poisonous treatment
Laughing at the new persona each one brought
Yet despising these plastic wigs and
All they meant

We cried together in your bed
At the future, knowing the unspeakable.
We planned and hoped for cures.
Deceitful thoughts.

We nursed you in your bed
Wrecked and eaten
Bathed you in the hope of washing it
All away.

We acknowledged the truth in your bed
You were going
We eased the pain with syringes of opiate
Sending you on your way.
You sucked the syringe like
A tiny bird.

We watched you slip away, slowly
In your bed
Your words laboured – few but powerful
Your face lined, old, yet so young

We decorated you with flowers in your bed
I lay with you
And felt your spirit transcend from your bed
Beauty – almost

After the funeral, at the gathering
The children jumped on your bed
Disrespectful pillow fights?
A boxing ring. Rather than
A shrine of death, laughter
Of life came from your bed.

Your husband lay prostrate with grief in your bed
He missed your skin, breathing, presence.
He mourned in your bed.

He and I sat on your bed,
Joined in grief
We fell into the pillows
We loved and temporarily relieved
Our pain with physical comfort.

Is this sacrilegious?
Is this the ultimate taboo?
Or is this union in your bed
The most natural of things?

Sometimes ghosts arrive at your bed
Is this you or my self-destructive nature
Riddled with guilt?

Chapter 5

Through the eyes of a child

Children will have their own perspective on love after death. Having seen one of their parents weep with sorrow at the death of their mum or dad, they may find it confusing that that parent could even think about moving on to a new relationship. They can feel a strong sense of anger, confusion, resentment, betrayal. 'How could they?' 'Have they forgotten my mum/dad?' 'Don't they still love them?' 'I don't need anyone to replace them – why do they?' A child may feel that they have lost part of themselves. These emotions are immense and can fester inside until they erupt. The surviving parent will be propelled forward by a new relationship, with its mixture of excitement and confusion. This can leave the child behind with nothing but loss.

In Shakespeare's *Hamlet*, Hamlet's mother remarries very soon after his father's death: 'But two months dead... Ere yet the salt of most unrighteous tears had left the flushing in her galled eyes, she married' (Act I, Scene II). Although others are judgemental of her, it is Hamlet, as her son, who feels most betrayed and hurt. He loves his father and idolises him in death. How could anyone else take his place? 'He is no more like my father than I to Hercules.' As he clings to the idea that his mother is still married to his father, he feels his mother is committing adultery with her new husband 'O, most wicked speed, to post with such dexterity to incestuous sheets. It is not, nor it cannot come to good.' He refuses to take off his mourning clothes for his mother's wedding and will not join in the celebrations.

This kind of reaction will be resonant for many widowed parents when they introduce a new partner into their children's lives. Lucia (see Lucia's story in Chapter 7, page 112) found that her daughter was very resistant to her new partner and did not want to know anything about him. The girl feels that her mother is married to her father and should not need anyone else. Her daughter actually admits that she would rather her mother remained alone and unhappy for the sake of her own happiness.

Tim (see Tim's story in Chapter 7, page 120) tells how all his children were very jealous initially: 'My eldest, Isabella, wanted me for herself. She was full of anger anyway, angry at life.' Sarah (see Sarah's story in Chapter 7, page 126), Tim's new partner, tells how Isabella tried to drive her away. She remembers how Isabella tried to control her younger brother and sister and prevent them from becoming close to her: 'There were times when they wanted to visit me and she forbade them from doing so. She told them I would never be their mummy.' It is as if Isabella was trying to hold on to the old order of her life. A child will be grieving for his or her family, as it was. They may feel this is in danger of being eroded further when a new person comes in. This can feel like a further loss and can shake their dependable feeling of 'home'.

This resentment from children can occur regardless of whether they are young or old. Esther (see Esther's story in Chapter 7, page 133) tells about her friend, whose wife was ill with cancer. When his wife died, he ended up forming a relationship with his wife's nurse. Her grown-up daughter would have nothing to do with this new relationship and was in fact obstructive. He was fifteen years older than his new love and he had multiple sclerosis (MS): 'You would have thought the family would have been delighted to have someone to look after him.' These obstructions meant that they ended up being married only a year before he died.

The confusion of grief

What is a child going through when they grieve? A child's grief is a very delicate area. It is extremely painful to see a child grieving, particularly your own. It may be essential to seek specialist help, as children may push away those who are closest to them. Winston's Wish (see Useful contacts) is an invaluable organisation that offers help for children and young people after the death of a parent, brother or sister. They offer support through their centre and an interactive website.

When a parent dies, there is no possibility of developing a more balanced relationship with them. Children are left with frozen, muddled, highly coloured fairytale memories. There may also be darker memories in the shadows that can cause guilty feelings even just thinking about them. There may be a feeling of resentment at being abandoned.

Even though glorification of the dead is a tendency common to everybody who is grieving, children may do this even more than adults. It is natural for young children to see no fault in their parents, but once a parent has died, they may idolise them even more. Their dead parent may always be remembered as perfect. As the child gradually begins to prepare to 'flee the nest', they will naturally begin to see faults with their living parent. This can be hard for the parent to live with. Following the death of her husband, Lucia tells how her teenage daughter has turned against her:

> I try to talk to her sometimes, but she goes mental at me. She has gone from being my lovely girl to being this horrible little b____
> … I cannot tell what is grief and what is teenage behaviour.

When a child has experienced a major trauma, it is difficult to unpick what causes certain behaviour. It is important to be aware of the danger of projecting our feelings on to the child.

Allowing a parent to move on

Although children may want to sabotage a new relationship and cling to the past, usually this will ease with time. Some children may actively want their living parent to find somebody new. Children have even been known to manoeuvre and introduce their parent to a potential new partner. When her father committed suicide, a seven-year-old made a poster asking for a new father only a few days later. Obviously, this could be seen as a reaction to trauma rather than a real desire. It is possible, however, that children could see finding a new parent as a way of mending everything that is broken. Some children are driven by a need to recreate a stable world.

Sarah tells how the youngest daughter of her new partner had created for herself, unprompted, a new inner family structure. When she had to do a school project on her family, she wrote: 'I live with my mum and dad and my big family. My mum died and we got involved with Sarah's family. I have two brothers and two sisters.'

There can be confusion and guilt if the new person is someone they get on with better than they did with their dead parent. The daughter of a widower remembers how, initially after her mother's suicide, she was resentful of her father having any relationships: 'We tore into little pieces the photos of his girlfriends.' Later, however, when he introduced one of his girlfriends as his new partner, she says:

> We recognised her from the photo. We did not mind. Actually we liked her. She was nice, a humorous, lively person, and she listened to us, unlike our mother in her last two years when she was really broken down.

Tim, a widower with three children, also talks about feeling guilty about life being easier. Speaking about his new relationship, he says: 'I think the children are having a more stable time, especially the little ones, than they ever had because Anya was very up and down.'

In experiencing this new stability and the happiness it can bring, children may have feelings that they are betraying their dead parent. The child may see the new person's presence in the house as a symbol of the betrayal. Claire (see Claire's story in Chapter 7, page 76), the new partner of a widowed father, says: 'When Vicky comes home, even now, I feel she would love it to be her mother at the cooker rather than me.' These feelings can be difficult to voice out loud, as the children may want to protect those around them.

Living alongside a child's needs

Even if children are not happy about their parent finding someone new, this has to be balanced with what is necessary for the adult. Marilyn (see Marilyn's story in Chapter 7, page 73) tells how her children:

...would not really like it if I had a new relationship, but if I was
happy, they would be happy. ...my son [told me] to make sure he
was a nice man. He said, anyway, he and his brother and sister
would look after me, saying I had no need of a man...

It is a lack of understanding of an adult's needs for a one-to-one relationship that leads to this dilemma. Kerri (see Kerri's story in Chapter 7, page
88) says:

It did feel funny at thirty-nine years old to be telling my son that
I had a boyfriend. At first he was shocked and a bit upset. I
explained to him: "Daddy's gone and Mummy gets very lonely
when you are in bed".

It is too much to expect a grieving child to understand their parent's emptiness and longing when they are trying to deal with their own.

When Sophie, the teenage daughter of Lucia reacted fiercely to her
mother having a new man around, Lucia pointed out that her friends with
divorced parents had to accept a new daddy. Sophie said: 'But their dad is
still alive. I just want to hold my daddy.' 'I want to hold your daddy too',
replied Lucia. They both want the same man to hug them, but Lucia
wants him as a husband while Sophie wants him as a father. It is beyond
Sophie's comprehension to understand how her mother, while still
wanting to hold her husband, could possibly want to hold another man:
'You are married, you are married to daddy...' Being a child, it is impossible to empathise with her mother's needs 'for one special person', least of
all her mother's sexual needs.

However, every parent's dilemma is how to juggle their own needs
with their children's. 'Children do not ask to be born. They are our
responsibility,' says Marilyn. On the other hand, is it right for Lucia's
daughter to demand that her mother should stay on her own? How does
the adult nourish their emotional needs? The theory is that a happy
parent is a happy child. What should a parent allow for themselves?
Where is the mid-point in this spectrum?

When a child has lost a parent, everyone is concerned about their
happiness. However, outsiders may often question the surviving parent's
behaviour in relation to the children. This can lead to value-based judgement. Elizabeth (see Elizabeth's story in Chapter 7, page 98), a widow,

was very adamant when she said: 'I fear for the children who have to adapt to seeing their parent in a new relationship before they have grieved.' Outsiders may see their role as ensuring that, in their grief, the parent does nothing rash that could hurt the children. Simon (see Simon's story in Chapter 7, page 80), a widower who moved on six months after his wife died, reports: 'People in the village actually said to me: "Isn't it a bit soon? What about the children?" When I reassured them that they were fine with it, they said, "That's alright then".'

Advice is given freely about how to treat the children and what is good for them, particularly about how to introduce the subject of a new partner. Lucia tells how '…one friend said "Get him in the house, Sophie has to get used to him." Another said keep him right away.'

A slow dawning

The introduction of a new person is a delicate subject. People find that it is often best to take this slowly as it gives the child time to adapt to their loss while the parent is determining what is going on with their new emotions. Kerri, a widow with two sons, states:

> I would not introduce [somebody new] unless I was absolutely certain. They got to know Mahmud as a friend at barbecues and picnics. It was a while before we told them that he was more than a friend.

When her son was told formally,

> At first, he was shocked and a bit upset… After a couple of days, Joshua asked to talk to me and said he was happy for Mahmud to be my boyfriend. He has been absolutely fine ever since and now wants to know whether we are going to get married.

Sarah says:

> We took it very slowly and did not put it right in front of them. We gave them the option of coming to terms with it slowly by not presenting it to them in unavoidable terms. We made sure they did not see us in bed together for a very long while. Until it felt right for all of us.

Likewise, Richard (see Richard's story in Chapter 7, page 100) said: 'The youngest one is fine. The oldest one had some teething problems. We have taken it very slowly.'

Parents may have to gauge how much of their new relationship they feel comfortable exposing to their children. Tim describes how his daughter, Isabella, was horrified to see him kissing Sarah after his wife died. Sarah discussed Isabella's horror with her own son, and his interpretation was that Tim was still wearing a wedding ring. When Sarah pointed out that Tim had never worn a wedding ring, her son replied: 'It is a wedding ring in his mind.' A few months later, when Isabella was warming to Sarah, Sarah's son explained that Isabella was less confused now, as Tim had 'taken the wedding ring off'. Eventually, Isabella was overheard in a conversation about mothers saying: 'Sarah is my mum now.'

All sorts of emotional shifts occurred to bring Isabella to this point. It helps when the new partner accepts the past and becomes active in bringing the dead parent into their everyday life. Sarah affirms the importance of doing this:

> We used to talk to the children about Anya [their mother] a great deal, because I felt it was important to keep her with us… We still have ceremonies where we remember her, like letting off balloons on her birthday, and we have her photograph in the living room… As our everyday lives have moved on, however, we seem to talk about her less, as they are grieving less.

Claire confirms this:

> The children go to visit [their mother's grave] less now. They had a very lovely time while she was alive. That's what you want to keep alive. You do not want to keep alive this hankering after what cannot be.

The new family

As their parent's new relationship becomes more of a reality, children will have to adjust to many changes in the structure of their lives. Children will have to adapt to this new world order. Everyone in it has to change the construct of how they view themselves. Elsie tells how, when her son-in-law remarried after her daughter's death, her grandson was told he would have to fit in to the new family. His father said he would not treat him any differently from the other children: 'I thought this was rather hard as he *is* different. He is *his* son and his mother is dead.' When you are young, your sense of self is linked strongly to your parents, so losing one parent means you lose some of your identity. Elsie's grandson's sense of identity is threatened: 'His mum will always be his mum. He will never call anyone else his mum...'

A childless widower coming together with a widow with two children, Mahmud (see Mahmud's story in Chapter 7, page 92) recognises this possible threat to a child's identity: 'Her husband will always be her children's father. I do not want to change their identity by making them take my name.' Her children also have to get used to someone who is not accustomed to having children around. Kerri, his partner, tells how '... we have our ups and downs, Mahmud is not used to having moody children around.' However, they adore this new adult in their lives as he is fun to be with and he gives them so much attention.

While in the midst of having to reconstruct their own world, other family members need to be sensitive to the children's needs. When her brother-in-law remarried after her sister's death, Agi was asked how she felt about the new family situation:

> Although some people expect me to feel unhappy about this, I am not. My sister is dead, nothing will bring her back and the children need a mother as much as their father needs a partner.

The turmoil of change

Change can bring its own grief. The new partner may have their own children, which can create jealousy and rivalry. There may be new rules, differences in ways of doing things, moving house, and so on. As a child goes through dealing with all these factors, a new inner picture of their new family will begin to emerge. This process will involve coming to terms with many internal questions. They have to work out what is 'allowed' in terms of thought and feeling:

- Is it alright to express their honest feelings about their dead parent?

- If they do, will it upset the remaining parent and the new partner once the 'cosy' new relationship has started?

- Can they talk to their friends about it?

- Do they want to talk to their teachers about it, or do they want to retain their school as an area of anonymity?

- Have they betrayed their dead parent by allowing this new person into their place?

- Is it wrong to feel close to the new partner?

- Would their dead parent have liked this new person?

- Is it wrong to feel, to laugh again, to feel normal? Or even to feel happier?

- Will they be allowed to celebrate anniversaries with the new person around?

These dilemmas will take a while to sort through. Some answers will be very personal, and the child will need to do their own working out. It is reassuring if an understanding adult can actively bring these questions out in the open. The time and place for discussion have to be gauged by the child's readiness and will require great sensitivity. No matter how open and honest their relationship is with their parent, the child may need a release valve. Counselling has proved invaluable for many children.

Addressing these confused feelings in a child can be quite a challenge for a new partner. Claire, who has children of her own, says that people are amazed how she has taken on three more children. She admits: 'I could not do this if the children did not get on.' Sarah feels that it is most important that:

> ...we have allowed the children time to blend together. They have set the pace and we have followed on behind... We feel like one big family with a few cracks.

The coming together of Tim's and Sarah's families presents an interesting synthesis of different perspectives. Sarah's children, who had been solely dependent on her for many years, expressed how their worst fear was their mother getting together with Tim and his family. Tim's children said *their* greatest fear was their mother dying. Sarah's children felt sorry for the girls: 'I feel that my children were incredibly generous in sharing me. They felt that the girls needed a mother.' Tim admits: 'At times, it feels as if Sarah is more bonded with *my* children than I am with *hers*.' This has changed now as he has more mental space because he is not grieving so much. If there can be a feeling of family, then it can start to fill up some of the emptiness of loss. One of Tim's happiest moments since his wife died was when:

> we were all in the car going off somewhere together. I really like that feeling... People see us as one big family. That makes me happy. Bringing it all together feels like an achievement.

Children have an innate ability to vacillate between extreme grief and a desire to play no matter what. One minute they can be distraught with grief; the next, they are demanding an ice-cream. Younger children particularly seem to possess an exceptional ability to live in the present, the here and now. They may have a more forthright attitude to what the adults are finding complicated. However, there are huge emotional tugs for children when seeing their parent move on. One positive thing about major trauma and its consequences is that children can emerge with a greater resilience.

The best situation children can find themselves in after losing a parent is one in which they are genuinely loved as part of a 'new' family. There is little else their natural parent would have wished for.

Children Speak Out
If someone dies, it doesn't mean you can't find love again.

You deserve to love again.

I don't think they should do it too fast, like the day after. Six months is alright.

A week later is a bit fast but it depends who the person is.

If they died of an illness and they didn't want to die, you might want to wait a while.
'How long is "a while"?'
'How long is a piece of string?'

We have to admit we weren't very happy when our parents got together. They were sneaking around behind our backs.

In the beginning, I was scared he was going to act like on the TV and get married straightaway to someone I didn't like. He promised he wouldn't do that.

I remember so clearly when we saw her putting sun cream on Daddy. We were so upset and we decided to have words with them.

I would withhold it from my children until I was sure but as soon as that was sure, I would tell them. Because children are bright.

I am not planning on my husband dying.

You can feel released if someone dies after they have been ill for a long, long time. It's a relief to get over the worry.

After Mum died, I hoped she would come back to life. Then I hoped that everything would be *exactly* the same, even though she wasn't there, that nothing would change, that the house would be the same.

I got really pissed off when I realised things were going to change. When Dad started to look at another woman after Mum died, I burnt her address. I was so annoyed and upset.

They started without telling us.

First I wanted Mum to come back… Then I wanted…a mum.

I was annoyed at first. Now I am OK with it. I like calling him funny names.

Maya found it annoying so I found it annoying too.

I honestly believe that it wasn't us that needed looking after. It was Daddy.

Later on, I realised it was the right thing. Mum would have wanted us to be happy.

I don't want them to get married.

I want them to get married.

I want to be a bridesmaid because it would be quite cool.

All us children coming together was really fun. It was OK. It was the best. I like all of us sleeping downstairs in the living room.

I've actually got someone who appreciates my jokes now.

It would be good if the grown-ups just went off.

It was hard for him when Mum died, but it was hard for us as well.

Sometimes you can be happier than before, for example if someone has been mean.

If they got married, I would feel really happy, but I can imagine some people might feel guilty feeling happy.

People tell me I am happier now. I like having a big family. I don't feel guilty feeling happy about that. It is a different situation.

I feel louder now we have a big family.

If you have enough of a heart, it is easy to take on other people's children.

It's not only because we have moved in that things have changed. It is because we are growing up.

It's OK to be happy after someone has died, otherwise life would be a total waste and a mess.

Chapter 6

Judgement

The world comes in

It appears that major life events such as birth, marriage and death lend themselves to people's opinions and judgement. The passion and emotional essence of these events evoke strong feelings and thoughts. These can be very positive and supportive, a coming-together of minds. Agi saw her sister's husband remarry after her death but appreciated the fact that his new partner had been her sister's best friend. She wrote to her:

> I know how much you loved her and what you did during her illness. I know how Anya loved you. I also feel it must be a terribly difficult situation to come into parallel to coming to terms with your own feelings.

Many uninvited opinions can easily be viewed as criticism, however, and can even become negative influences. At such raw times as grieving, feelings can be amplified and magnified. This leaves the bereaved person open and vulnerable to the comments and attitudes of others. It is such an entirely personal and solitary process. No outsider can understand fully the choices and decisions made by the bereft. However, it has to be admitted that sometimes people do make desperate choices through sheer loneliness.

Should anyone judge another person? Concern is natural, but where does the line between care and interference fall? In *Men and Grief* (1991), Staudacher states categorically: 'A man who married relatively soon after his wife's death will almost certainly be the one who has not gone through the normal grieving process.' She suggests that this grief will be inhibited or suppressed. She talks of a 'retreating phase', which includes shock and disbelief and then real grief-related emotions.

Even if true, value-based judgements can cut like a knife through the heart of the griever, an already damaged heart at that. A widowed psychotherapist, Elizabeth (see Elizabeth's story in Chapter 7, page 98) states: 'In my opinion, if people form a new relationship too soon, it does not bode well for the future.' She criticises a well-known female celebrity for starting a new relationship during her husband's long illness, 'even before her husband died'. She considered this to be 'male behaviour'. This celebrity, however, understands why people criticise but said: 'It is so personal. I just knew where I was in my own grief.' Her mother's, sister's and then her husband's death from cancer made her 'realise the need to take the good things in life when they come along'.

This type of thinking assumes that all people are exactly the same, that they all have experienced the same type of loss within the same time span. In fact, there are so many variable factors:

- Was the loss sudden, traumatic?
- Was the loss through a managed illness?
- Had the griever spoken of death?
- Had the griever given permission for their partner to move on?
- Was there denial?
- Did they have a loving relationship before the death?

These and many other factors cause the bereaved person to experience their loss in their own unique way.

As discussed in Chapter 1, although there is a cycle to grief, there is no correct way to pass through this cycle. Even people who have been bereaved themselves find it hard not to pass judgement on how others should go through this cycle. Harry, a participant in a hospice support group, relates the story of a desperate man in his group: 'All he did was cry. He did not say a word.' When the man did not come back to the group, Harry fearfully telephoned him to find out how he was. He had booked a cruise with a new love 'just two months after his wife died'. There was a sense of shock among the other group members. They felt that it was impossible that he could have grieved and recovered so fast. However, they did acknowledge that their judgement was clouded by their own feelings: their already fragile minds were stirred up and unsettled by his actions.

In Mahmud and Kerri's stories (Chapter 7, pages 88–98), they report that even though their bereavement group was totally invaluable to them, they found other members to be very judgemental about their new relationship. Mahmud notices how, although people grieve at different rates:

> They use where they were, say at six months, as a benchmark and expect others to be at the same point. If you are further ahead than they were at this time, they will say: 'I'm worried about you because when I was [at] six months, I had a breakdown.'

However, he found that the judgement of other bereaved people was more acceptable than that passed by outsiders. Maybe they were not blaming or judging him, but they just could not understand it in their own terms. In grief, it is possible for two people to be at different ends of a spectrum and for others to be somewhere in between.

As friends and family move at a different pace from the widowed person, they can often be censorious when they see signs of moving on. This can be just little things like changes in the home. Sue, who saw her dead friend's husband remarry, tells of her surprise when all the photographs of her friend were taken down. She felt as though her friend was being banished, and she judged this to be wrong behaviour.

Uninvited opinion versus concern

On 4 May 2004, two very contrasting articles were written about comedian Paul Merton's marriage. Paul Merton had lost his wife, Sarah, to breast cancer in September 2003 and married Suki in April 2004. In her article in the *Evening Standard*, 'How Soon is Too Soon?', Amanda

Platell asks: 'Isn't it all a bit soon, Paul? How can a man hold one love in his arms as she dies then hold another only months later?' Talking about her own widowed sister-in-law who, eight years on from her brother's death, is still grieving, she says: 'He is the only one she ever wanted to grow old with.' This is a painful value-based judgement. It may be so that this is the way for her sister-in-law, but why should it be the same for Paul Merton? 'It seems a little hasty to me', she comments. Since it is not her experience, how could she know?

On the same day, Susan Quilliam wrote an article in the *Daily Express* entitled 'Why I believe Paul Merton is ready for love in his life'. In this, she acknowledged that there is a danger in taking on a new relationship when 'one is still reeling from the loss of the old'. She recognises that this can lead to the grieving process being arrested, leaving the person unwilling to really care and to recommit. However, she feels Paul Merton's grieving process was well under way when Sarah died. This process would have commenced from the moment of diagnosis nineteen months before the end of her life. This allowed them to face the end together and helped Paul to grieve pre-emptively. She comments that the daily struggle of the illness 'makes him need to take a little now rather than give'. Quilliam assumes that during the final months, Sarah would have told Paul to be happy and to enjoy being with someone else. The contrast between these articles is significant. It is indicative of the spectrum of opinion. Judge not. We do not know.

> The soul walks not upon a line
> Neither does it grow like a reed
> The soul unfolds itself like a lotus of countless petals.

(Gibran 1997)

Facing the taboo

The issue of judgement has been raised in each story in Chapter 7 of this book. Everyone has received opinions and criticisms, clearly showing that somehow the subject of love after death is a minefield. They are venturing into an awkward area, one that exists in almost all cultures, albeit affecting mainly women. Why is it that society finds this threatening? If a person has married, then they have made a statement to the world. Perhaps this is why the world feels it has ownership of their behaviour afterwards? It is astonishing, however, that in these days of liberation of thought and behaviour, this taboo still exists.

People deal with this judgement in varying but similar ways. They seem to develop their own inner feelings of what is right and wrong in their attempt to defend themselves. Marilyn (see Marilyn's story in Chapter 7, page 73) is a widow who comes from the Philippines. She tells how a woman in her village remarried one month after her husband's death: 'This shocked the fishing village... However, I say it all depends on the person.' Rachel, an older widow (see Rachel's story in Chapter 7, page 85), says:

> I felt as if everybody was talking round me and arranging my life, and I just did not want this. Everyone had opinions. 'Too soon' was a common one.

'It is not only other people's judgement ... I judge myself', says Sarah (see Sarah's story in Chapter 7, page 126). She felt uncomfortable with the feeling that the world was judging her relationship with her friend's husband so soon after her friend's death. She felt, however, that for her partner, Tim, this was not an issue: 'He did not notice or he did not care. Maybe it was just men closing doors quicker. I think some of his friends found his ease shocking.'

Esther (see Esther's story in Chapter 7, page 133) found that people were very judgemental when she started a relationship with a man recently widowed:

> [They] rejected me and would not talk to me. It was not me that was having a relationship so soon after losing a spouse. It was him. But some people would have nothing to do with me.

Throughout this chapter, it has become very clear that the world does judge. It is inescapable. However, whatever people say, it is apparent that this transition into love after death is an intensely personal experience. Although people can feel governed by what is expected, this may be in conflict with their own direct experience. This can lead to inner battles. But the value of instinct and intuition should never be underestimated.

Your soul is oftentimes a battlefield upon which your reason and
your judgement wage war against your passion and your appetite.

(Gibran 1997)

Into the Hour
I have come into the hour of a white healing.
Grief's surgery is over and I wear
The scar of my remorse and of my feeling.

I have come into a sudden sunlit hour
When ghosts are scared to corners, I have come
Into the time when grief begins to flower

Into a new love. It had filled my room
Long before I recognized it. Now
I speak its name. Grief finds its good way home.

The apple-blossom's handsome on the bough
And Paradise spreads round. I touch its grass.
I want to celebrate but don't know how.

I need not speak though everyone I pass
Stares at me kindly. I would put my hand
Into their hands. Now I have lost my loss

In some way I may later understand.
I hear the singing of the summer grass.
And love, I find, has no considered end,

Nor is it subject to the wilderness
Which follows death. I am not traitor to
A person or a memory. I trace

Behind that love another which is running
Around, ahead. I need not ask its meaning.

(Jennings 2002)

Chapter 7

People's stories

In the following stories, real experience is shared, and it is possible to see various battles and triumphs. Individual reactions to the challenges of grief and change show the depth of human resilience. All these people say that they have learnt not so much about death but about living.

Marilyn's story

Marilyn is from the Philippines and has been a widow since her husband was killed sixteen years ago. She has three children and has not remarried.

My husband, Rosauro, was killed just before my birthday. He sent a card in advance. He always knew he would die, and so did I. He believed in and fought for his cause and was known as Ka-ex, which was his revolutionary name. He was fighting with the Communists against Iquino's regime. I had been expecting it to happen because we had been victims of abuse of power. We thought Iquino would change all, as she had promised, but we were disillusioned.

When he died, I had to ignore my feelings because we had nothing and I had to work immediately. My children were seven, six and four. I really wanted to die at that point. I hadn't seen him for two to three months, but I was sad at the finality of it all. He was ambushed on his way back home. I used to cry and get angry if I saw a government soldier, but

now I realise that their wives would feel the same loss if their husbands
were killed. My husband said you cannot fight without blood and you
have to make a stand. Now I don't believe in fighting.

We were called to identify his body but I could not recognise him. We
identified him only by his toe and a mark on his body. Because of his
injuries, we had to have a closed coffin. Normally, the coffin is open in the
Philippines. My children would not believe he was really dead because
they had not seen him, but I wanted to protect them. We all wore white at
the funeral rather than the normal black, because we still believed in the
cause. We were proud of him.

My youngest is very like his father, even the way he runs. The revolu-
tionaries want him to join them in the fight. They expect something from
me and my family. My husband, though, had said that he did not want
any of us to follow his footsteps. He was a hero, heroic in his public life,
but to me he was just a normal man.

My husband was always away so I do not know if I ever felt married.
When he returned, there was always fear around that he would be hunted.
I sometimes wish he had gone off with another woman rather than died.

I remember the way he courted me was with a serenade. It is the
custom in my country. He played the guitar and sang beautifully. He told
me that he would have serenaded me even if I had been already married.
He had to convince me to marry him because I never really wanted to
marry because of the way my father was. We were married for nine years. I
have a tape of him singing with my children. It is the only thing I have, as
we lost everything when we had to flee after he died.

I did not want to grieve. I could not, anyway, because we just had to
find ways to survive. In the Philippines, the normal way of mourning is
one year of wearing black, no dancing, singing or laughing out loud.
Women are supposed to sit inside the house doing nothing. The men are
not expected to do the same. In fact, people expect them to get married
again quickly, especially if they have children.

My children are everything to me. I have to hold back. They did not
ask to be born and they are my responsibility. I am human and I am
attracted at times to men. It is normal, I am a woman. But I hold back.
There was someone once, but we were different religions and I feared this
would come between us. I do not really want to have to look after a man

again. I have freedom now and I am independent. I can go anywhere. No one will question me. It is not wrong to fall in love again, but the children are my main reason for living. I would be worried that a new man would not wholeheartedly support my children. I do not rely on men. I never have done, because my father gave nothing to my mother. As my husband was always away as an outlaw, I had to be independent.

My children would not really like it if I had a new relationship, but if I was happy, they would be happy. I was talking to my son about how it would be if I remarried. He said he would rather I did not, but, if I had to, to make sure he was a nice man. He said, anyway, he and his brother and sister would look after me, saying I had no need of a man. I have not really spoken to them about it much. I still feel married to my children.

I do not feel that I am still married to my husband. I believe that, when we die, we will meet again. But we will not be married. I still wear my wedding ring because I have been married. I am happy this way. If it is a nice man who is interested in me, he should not be put off by my wedding ring. My friends say I am silly and should take it off. They think I should get a new man. I am happy for other widows who have formed a relationship. A woman in my village married after one month, purely because of her child. This shocked the fishing village and they compared us. I say it all depends on the person.

As a widow trying to support three children, I found myself in vulnerable situations with men. Sometimes I wished I could die. After two years, I had to go to Saudi Arabia to earn money for the family to survive financially. It was terrible to leave my young children. My daughter had to become the mother to my two boys. While I was there, the man of the house tried to rape me. I made him stop by singing. I cried for a week. I could not tell my children or my friends why. I felt they could do anything they liked to you, even throw you out of the window.

I do look back at the past but have to accept the present. My faith has helped me. Love is not just about my husband. I can love in other ways.

ᕦ

Claire's story

Claire was divorced with one daughter. She is now married to Simon, the husband of a friend. They are both in their forties.

I met Simon and Julia when our children were at school together. I had been to their house several times for dinner. Then Julia was diagnosed with ovarian cancer in the autumn and died the next May. I did not see her during her chemotherapy, so my main memories are of her being vivacious and beautiful.

I think she wanted Simon to go ahead and meet someone else and not remain in that grey period too long. Other people tell me she would be very pleased for the children. My friends, having seen me alone for so many years, are happy for me to have found someone. So, in a way, it has not all been a waste. It obviously has been a huge waste in that a life was lost, but good has come out of it.

I felt initially I should not be here. It should be Julia. If we were really happy in an intimate situation, I suddenly felt: 'This should not be.' Simon was so much more pragmatic. He took pains to tell me that she and I were so different. The good thing is that, as he and I were older, we were more experienced and therefore more relaxed in intimate situations. Many people wondered how I could take on board so much. Julia and Simon had three children and I had two. If the children had not got on, I could not have done it. I had gone through a divorce, which had been shocking because I really felt I had married for life. I had felt abandoned.

Julia is still around sometimes, either spiritually or in my head, although this is less now. Once, when I was at a Van Morrison concert with Simon and his daughter, I suddenly remembered how much they both loved this music and I burst into tears. I felt she was present there, sitting between us. I do believe that when people die, they are here for a while until they are ready to move on, or until you are ready to let them move on. It is as if they want to see that everything is fine. One of the things which allowed us not to have her with us all the time was Simon being so comfortable and guilt-free about putting things where they belong.

Another reason Simon felt able to move on quickly was that he was so busy living her death and he did his grieving as she was dying. There must be such a difference with a sudden death, like a car crash. Simon was also used to death in a way because he had had so many deaths amongst his family and friends. Although this does not prepare you, he was not a stranger to death.

They were the perfect family. They had these three beautiful children and they were the centre of the village social scene. Then this awful thing happened to them. For these lovely children to lose their lovely mummy was devastating. It was a perfect picture cracked in half.

When I moved in to his house, there were pictures of Julia everywhere. It was difficult. Maybe it was a mistake. This was the only query my mother ever had about the situation. I had a particularly difficult situation with the extension. Julia and Simon had been building one and it was only finished after she died. They had planned a big house-warming for it, and Simon and I thought we should have it anyway. It was six months after she died. All these people came along who had been very much Julia's friends. Some of them did not come at all and some of them left early. They found it very difficult. They found it difficult to be celebrating at a party without her.

It was difficult to move her photos. In our bedroom, there was a black-and-white photograph of their wedding, where they looked young and beautiful. I found it particularly difficult. Simon had not even realised the implication. I found the best way to change this was to decorate the room and the things just did not go back in.

The children have photographs, particularly Vicky, who was seventeen when her mother died. She has photographs all over her walls. Her reaction has been different from her brothers'. They busied themselves and are pretty happy. Yes, they have a big loss, but they do not talk about her so much. For Vicky, it is like a huge wound which will never go away but just becomes more comfortable, more bearable.

Simon does still wear his wedding ring. Admittedly, things like that do bug you. He did, however, have a whole life with her and you cannot suddenly say: 'Sorry, it's me now.' Some people do that after a divorce. It is as though the previous partner did not exist. That can be difficult for the children. I am sure he still loves her. You do not just stop. Maybe he is not in love with her in the same way as he was. But it is alright for him to love her. In fact, I am the one who puts flowers on her grave most often.

The children go to visit her grave less now. They had a very lovely time while she was alive. That's what you want to keep alive. You do not want to keep alive this hankering after what cannot be. It is not very productive. When Vicky comes home, even now, I feel she would love it to be her mother at the cooker rather than me. There is something about the cooker and the heart of the home.

When my own daughter and I happen to be in the house alone together, there is a different feeling in the air. We have a great history together and she has seen me in worse times. She knows me differently. But we are one family with Simon and his children. My daughter feels that my marrying Simon has been a godsend. The day we got married, she voiced her relief that someone else was looking after me.

Bereavement is, in one way, easier than divorce for children because they can carry on thinking that Mummy and Daddy loved each other more than anything else in the world. They can feel confident in this, whereas in divorce they can feel rejected and that something has gone wrong. Looking back, I am so pleased that loneliness has gone.

I went to Julia's funeral. The church was so full and it was a beautiful sunny day. I saw Simon and I thought he looked so amazing. It was like he had an aura around him. He held his head up high. After she died, Simon had more cottage pies than he could possibly want delivered to his door. People were very kind and were trying to help him hold it all together. Several local women propositioned him. He resisted and now feels glad he did not allow himself to be comforted this way. A while after the funeral, about five months, I thought I would love to give him a call. After our first date, he said that *he* would have phoned *me* up eventually. There was obviously something in the air. I do not think I felt sorry for him or was thinking about his children. I just saw him as a man. I was sure it was something I wanted. I did not want to travel this world on my own, although I am sure there are people who are happy doing so.

When we first were together, I don't think he was openly grieving but he had bouts of it. Things would trigger his grief. It helped that we got off on a good footing. I really like his family. They have similar tastes and values to my family. Julia had not got on with them so, for him, this was a huge 'levitation'. His mother said I was like a breath of fresh air. This made me feel valued. She had also said to Simon when we first met: 'She will do very nicely.'

This gave me the confidence to walk in on what everyone viewed was a 'perfect family'. I would have expected the children to have been asking 'Why? Why? Why?' questions. However, I think they did not seem to be confused, because Julia and the family had very much managed her death. The weekend that they knew she was going to die, they brought her home from the hospital and they drank champagne. Although they all saw her physically deteriorating and losing her hair, I feel the image of her will always be that of beauty. For Simon, she will always be a forty-year-old woman, whereas *I* will grow old – hopefully.

The fact that Simon and I have had to go straight into being parents together makes us look forward to the time when the children have grown up. It is the reverse of what happens when you marry and have children young. This parenting takes our time. Simon has the wisdom that comes from life experience and is good with the children. At the same time, he can still be playful.

Friends of Simon felt their role was altered, having previously been comforters and supporters. They were quite put out when I came along. Perhaps they even wanted to be in my position, although they knew they could not be. There were one or two people who said: 'Good for you. We wish you all the happiness.' One woman came around when I was cooking and said how nice it must be for Simon to come back to the smell of cooking in the house. The same person also gave me a good piece of advice: she said that Julia had never been interested in the garden and that it could be something I could make my own. Everything I have done in the garden is all me and Simon. Most importantly, she said to Simon: 'Go out and buy a new bed.' Things like this are fundamentally important. Simon would never have thought about that. Men do not necessarily feel these things.

We do not see Julia's family. They are quite distant people. It is disappointing, as children need grandparents. Julia's mother died of cancer and maybe her father still has not recovered from losing a wife and a daughter. Simon took his youngest up there last year, but it would be nice if he came down here. Maybe his father-in-law feels it would be an intrusion if he did because of our new relationship.

We are really happy now, and when the children come home, the house is full of these big bodies and life. They all get on so well and they are all such full characters. Simon has always made me feel really good about coming into this tricky situation.

Simon's story
Simon is a widower with three children. He married Claire, a mutual friend. They are both in their forties.

I think the person who has had the hardest job has been Claire. *She* is the person that needs congratulating. It is a very delicate situation coming in on a bereaved family. We were a family in a mess. You think you are the most important because you have been bereaved and you are grieving. When it comes down to it, it could be turned the other way. Claire could equally feel bereft. Coming into this situation, you are taking on something which needs fixing. All sorts of unexpected questions come up, like when do you kiss the other person's children goodnight? It is very easy to make mistakes and hurt someone.

Claire experiences a lot more than I actually realise. I do not think blokes go through it so much. They do not think too much, really, particularly physically. They act before they think rather than think before they act sometimes. Although that was not our case. I knew this was something special so I took my time so as not to spoil anything.

It helped a great deal when the children's school mentioned Julia's illness in assembly and asked the other children to pray for her. For the children, the fact that there has been death in the family, with all of the awfulness about it, is not as bad as a divorce, as it is nobody's 'fault'. There is a legacy problem in divorce, which means you have to continue managing a difficult situation. With a death, you manage a decreasingly difficult situation. They can see that everyone can continue loving each other.

When my wife died, I used to go out in the car with the music full on and cry out loud. Now, I find it curious that I do not think of her very often. I feel that Julia has not gone but that she is in the next room, like in that lovely poem (see 'Death is Nothing At All', pp.29–30). We can visit that room whenever we want, but we do so less and less.

The period of her illness is just a blur. I was in coping mode. It was a managed illness as she was ill for a long time, which is different from sudden death. That is when people really need to be given space and perhaps would not find it so easy to move on to another relationship. Not being able to say goodbye would be just so terrible. For me, I think I got off lightly. If I had not been there during her illness, it would have been a scar for a long time.

Only now can I look at videos. I do not actively want to do it. I don't think I glorify Julia now she is dead. I have even criticised her to Claire, but it is a natural thing for the human brain to select all the good memories over the bad. I didn't put her on a pedestal, but I think you polarise your thoughts. The good stuff can seem fantastic and the bad stuff even worse. The grey stuff in the middle, which is actually day-to-day life, you forget. If you can do this, it puts into perspective and compartmentalises what has gone before. Thought processes trigger other thoughts; therefore, if you think of sad things, you will remember the sad stuff. If you think of good things, you will remember the good stuff. You can actively use it to your advantage to help you as a device. Occasionally, I can feel sad when I look at happy photographs, and there are certain tracks and hymns I cannot listen to.

When Claire and I started going out, people in the village actually said to me: 'Isn't it a bit soon? What about the children?' When I reassured them that they were fine with it, they said 'That's alright then.'

Getting married in the church where we had had Julia's funeral was risky. People who had some anxiety about us getting married at all and who hadn't moved with us in the relationship were also there. The last time they had been in that church was at the funeral. We questioned whether this was a wise move, but our local vicar assured us that death is part of life and the fact that all these things took place in that church was a good thing. It took a lot of guts, particularly for Claire, to go ahead there. We also asked the kids and they were alright about it. You have to make judgement calls. Some things are going to hurt other people. The most important thing was that we were the family unit, the six of us. Vicky sang beautifully for us. Something very beautiful happened spiritually, although our wedding was very tough for quite a few people.

One of the worst things about our wedding was that the best man leant too much on the past. In his speech, he said: 'Julia is here with us and she is looking down and she is really pleased.' I looked round and there were tables of Julia's best friends in tears and looking so mournful. Claire felt that everyone was just about holding together a situation that was harder for them than for us. This speech evoked too much emotion. This took away from the happiness of getting married. That was a tough one. The vicar dealt with it better by saying: 'These two people who have seen a lot more of life than some of us here…' We all knew she was there. We did not need the best man to spell it out.

We always think of Julia partying away up in Heaven. It makes me feel better to think that there is a spirit up there who knows what is going on. I can't imagine the three of us in Heaven. Claire sometimes thinks about how Julia would still be young and beautiful, whereas she would be old.

Both of us feel very lucky to have been given a second chance. Second love is very different from the first. You have learnt things in one relationship which you can put into practice in the second. I feel a bit cheated that I have missed out on our honeymoon because of the children. We are looking forward to having time together once the children have grown.

Anne's story
Anne is a young, childless widow, now in a new relationship.

My husband, Paul, was diagnosed in April with cancer. It was already a secondary tumour. He had died by August. He was thirty-eight when he died and I was thirty-six. We had been married twelve years. Our wedding anniversary was in the intensive care unit, and the nurses kindly made a cake for us. Our lives had been so busy; we had no children. Chemotherapy brought home to Paul this absence in our lives. He said: 'It's done in my chances for kids.' My mum said it would be better if we had had them because I would not be left on my own. But I think it must be more difficult if you do. I like children…I am a teacher.

I know Paul wouldn't want me to spend the rest of life on my own. When he was dying, we didn't talk about his death or about my future. I wonder about this now. I was never sure how much he knew. The lowest point was when he said: 'I don't know whether I am going to see my next birthday and I don't want to leave you.'

At the worst times, I thought I was going round the bend. What helped me was writing things down. As time has gone on, I write in my diary less than I did. The other thing that helped was an organisation called 2Higher Ground. They offer life coaching for cancer carers and people who have lost someone to cancer. They seem to focus more on how to move on and practical things, rather than going over the past. One of the worst things for me was money. He had always handled this. I did not know what to do for the best.

After Paul died, I became very active. I went white-water rafting, joined an adventure group and lived at the gym. I only had myself to worry about. The month after he died, I went to the hospital and I asked the palliative care people if they knew of any dating agencies. I felt dreadful as it was so soon after, but all my friends were in couples. I know it was an odd idea, but I just wanted someone to go out to the pub with. They sent me to an agency which sounded reputable, which I joined. It was a bit nerve-wracking. I hadn't done this sort of thing since I was twenty. That's how I met Steve. My parents don't know how I met him. I don't know what they would make of it. Sometimes I thought: 'What the hell am I doing?' I felt a lot of guilt. How could I lose Paul and want to try and move on so quickly?

Steve was the third person I met through the agency. He was single. On our first date, I felt so guilty. I just wanted life to go back to how it was when I was married. I wanted somebody there. After we first slept together, I thought: 'What am I doing? I am too old to start all over again. This is what you do in your early twenties. I don't know the rules any more.' When we met, Steve asked me: 'Were you looking for anything in particular in somebody?' I wasn't. I was prepared to meet anybody. It is difficult not to compare, but they are totally different.

I didn't tell anybody about meeting Steve for quite a while, as I was worried what they were going to think. When I told my parents, they were relieved that I had found somebody else. They had been worried about me being on my own. My best friend thought it was wonderful. Paul's family still don't know. They never really accepted me. When Paul went into hospital, I saw them there every day and it was hard work talking to them.

Steve and I have had our ups and downs, some of which were to do with me being a widow. I still had things to sort out, such as Paul's ashes and his things. Steve has been very good. He has never prevented me from talking about Paul. He said he does not want me to deny my past. He was really threatened in the early days, but not now. It helps that Steve understands what it is like to lose someone, as he lost his parents early and then his oldest brother.

I think bereavement is more difficult for men because they don't talk like women do. They feel they have to put on a brave face. I suppose *I* have had to put on a brave face. I had to protect my mum, who would worry too much about me if I said I wasn't OK. Friends are the best, particularly girlfriends...

I know it's a taboo to speak ill of the dead, and when I made a negative comment about Paul, my mum was shocked. But he could be a pain in the neck, and so could I. I remember him warts and all. Outsiders can be shocked about this.

Steve and I have been talking about wills recently and I told him how I wanted my ashes to be scattered in two different places, one spot with Steve and one spot with Paul. Perhaps as years go on, I might change...

Every day, I think of something about Paul. When I finally lost one of our cats through cancer, the one he had called his 'cancer buddy', it was awful. It triggered something. I don't feel that Paul is around, but there are still so many possessions around that we bought together and *these* make him present. A lot of my memories are of places we went to. I keep photographs of him in my study. Steve is happy with this. On holiday, I found a ring which only fitted my wedding-ring finger and I put the new ring on that finger. It's a difficult one. I am not really married any more but...

Even now, there are certain things I can't talk about to Steve. There are days when I feel I would like to go back to life as it was and then realise I can't. When I feel like this, I feel guilty for poor Steve. However, things are getting better as our life has changed and we have moved

house. I still think some days: 'Why can't life be easy?' But I feel lucky to
have somebody to put up with me and to have Steve there.

Rachel's story

Rachel was widowed young. Her Orthodox Jewish faith required her to participate
in a specific ceremony before marrying her new husband. They were married for
many years before he died. She is now eighty.

When my husband, Saul, died twelve years ago, I felt I had lost my best
friend. We were parted in life but not in love. He was still here. I kept
wanting to tell him things. When I thought of something that made us
laugh, I'd think: 'Oh, I must just tell him.' We were married getting on for
forty years.

There are many rituals that help you adapt to losing somebody in the
Jewish religion. We gather round for *Shiva* and sit together for prayers
every night. Some people say it does not help, but I felt it did. Having
people around helps. The *Shiva* is a week long and, after that, you start
picking up the pieces. The official period of mourning is one year, but you
can marry any time after that. I know someone who met someone at the
Shiva of her husband and, the moment she got up, she became engaged.
Most unusual. Men do move on quicker, but that's men of course. People
like you to marry; a rabbi said: 'People are not meant to be alone.'

I was married before when I was twenty-three years and the war had
just ended. From very early on, there was something wrong with
Benjamin. He was not taken on in the war. He went into hotel work,
something he really wanted, but he got ill so suddenly. It was terrible and
I was really sad. Benjamin died eighteen months after we married. My
mother hoped I would find someone else. I was shocked by this. When
Benjamin was ill, my mother was talking to someone who liked me. She
said: 'If you wait, you can have her.' I was furious and so was my friend.
We never spoke to each other again. My mother was forever introducing
me to people. I said: 'Do you mind? If I'm going to find someone, I'll find
him on my own.' Matchmaking is in the Jewish culture. I felt as if everybody was talking round me and arranging my life, and I just did not want

this. Everyone had opinions. 'Too soon' was a common one. But now, at the age of eighty, there is no such thing as 'too soon'.

I did not keep up with Benjamin's friends because the war was on. It was a period of comings and goings, and people were on the move or getting killed. There was more widowhood around. We used to go to youth clubs and you would meet men. Then they would go off to the forces and never come back. It was difficult to tell who was a widow and who was not at that time.

When I first met Saul, he asked me out and I said no. Perhaps I was thinking of my first husband, but I don't really know why I said no. I just wanted to get on with my teaching. I loved my teaching: it was my life. Saul found me again a few months later, and that was that.

When Saul and I wanted to marry five years later, he wanted to get married in an Orthodox synagogue. As I had been married before, we had to get permission and go through a ritual called *Halitzah*. Traditionally, a brother-in-law was expected to marry his brother's widow if she was childless; *Halitzah* is a ritual which releases him from this obligation. A difficult ritual, although I knew it was the right thing to do if I wanted children. We had to do it properly. My brother-in-law said: 'What a nonsense! I'm not going to be bothered with that.' But the rabbi said: 'I do not remember you being asked. You were told.' I had to spit at his feet, which is symbolic of saying 'You can go and take a running jump.' Something I felt like doing anyway. It was just a step that needed to be taken.

It was very strange being with someone else, especially in the beginning, at the wedding and everything. You think back. It was the ceremony that made me think back, even though it was quite different. We did not get married in the same synagogue; that would have been very strange. I never compared Saul and Benjamin. They were entirely different.

I still think of Benjamin – I still think of him. It's a long time ago, and it was all so quick. I did not feel in the least bit disloyal to him when I met Saul, though. I still see my old sister-in-law at the synagogue, but she does not know my new husband. My first husband's mother was very sweet about us. I kept in touch for a while. There is a wonderful photograph of her holding my second husband's baby. I do not have anything from that time. I don't think he ever gave me anything. I did have a wedding ring, but I put it on the other hand when I got married to Saul. Eventually, I disposed of it. It fell off. But life has to go on I suppose. I was still quite young.

I did not talk about Benjamin to Saul. I don't think he was interested. He used to make jokes: 'You've done two; maybe you'll make it three.' He was always pulling my leg. It just did not seem relevant to mention him. Saul also used to joke and ask me who I'd choose to be with in Heaven. I would just say: 'Ah, that would be telling.' He never referred to Benjamin, apart from the jokes. I feel he was very sure about our relationship. He never asked me about my past. He did meet Benjamin's mother once, but the two mothers-in-law did not get on.

I used to have photographs of Benjamin, but my mother threw all the old stuff away when she moved house. It was a long time before I realised the pictures had gone. I don't regret not having a photograph of him now. Maybe my mother was helping me move on. I have ones of Saul, of course.

I have not thought about Benjamin for a long time. I have no need to think of him. He was a very nice man, but I can't even remember what he looked like. It was such a long time ago.

When Saul died, it did not bring back memories of losing Benjamin. I was so wrapped with Saul and it had been forty years. I feel that now I would never have a new relationship. I'm eighty now, although I was in my late sixties when Saul died. There are some women who are never without a man. Even in their nineties, they have to have a man around. They have to be connected, I suppose. If I did meet someone, I would have to know I was definitely attached to them to be able to move away from Saul. It does not occur to me, I'm not interested… But then you never know what's round the corner.

Saul was an extremely kind man and very protective, which made it difficult because I had to learn to manage when he died. He was one of those men who held your hand when you were crossing the road. It is hard to learn to cope on your own. Maybe it was wrong that he was so protective, but he was protective of his mother and that was what he knew how to do.

Anyway, what has to be has to be. After a long marriage, I don't want to have a new relationship. Saul was the main part of my life. He filled up my life.

Kerri's story

Kerri is a young widow with two children in a relationship with Mahmud, a childless widower. He has recently lost his wife.

My husband, Ian, was on a six-week tour in South America with some friends, trekking on the Inca Trail. He died of a heart attack two days before he was going to come home. It was a shock because he was very, very fit. It was totally out of the blue. We were teenagers when we met, and he was my first boyfriend. We had been married thirteen years, and we had Joshua, who had just turned six, and a six-week-old baby. We had chosen while I was on maternity leave for him to go away. It had been a lifelong ambition and I was not going to stand in his way. The only thing that makes this thing bearable is that he actually achieved his ambition. He was thirty-six when he died.

After my father died and I was having to care for my suicidal mother, we had decided to have another baby, because we did not know how life would turn out. We did not want Joshua to be an only child should the unthinkable ever happen. I went into postnatal depression the day the baby was born. Ian was due to go on the trip and I insisted he went even though he had doubts about leaving me.

After Ian died, I just went into overdrive. You either curl up and die, shut yourself away like my mum did, or you get up and you keep going for the children's sake. If I didn't look after them, nobody would. You don't have a choice. When the kids were in bed, I would do my crying and my grieving. Josh did not want to see his mummy crying, so I didn't, for his sake.

About eighteen months later, I found Winston's Wish, which is the centre for bereaved children. They suggested the WAY Foundation, which stands for 'widowed and young', for me. I actually became their press officer because I wanted other people to get what I got out of it. It has been a lifeline. Mahmud and I met at a work meal and coincidentally he was also a member of WAY.

Before I met Mahmud, Ian's family used to say: 'You need to get out and meet somebody,' and I answered: 'How the hell am I going to meet someone pushing a pram around the park?' It just was not going to happen. It did not cross my mind that I would meet somebody while the children were young. It was not that I did not want to. Although I loved Ian to bits, I was very lonely. Mahmud and I met and got on instantly. He had lost his wife about two months earlier from a brain haemorrhage. It took us a month or so before we started seeing each other. It took me by surprise when I started to have feelings for somebody again. As I had been with Ian since I was eighteen, I could not imagine being in a relationship with someone else.

It was confusing getting together. I did not know whether it was him I liked or the attention. He is a caring guy, totally different from Ian. I realised it wasn't only the attention; it was Mahmud I was attracted to. The night I met Ian, we knew there was going to be something special. He said something and I laughed back. When I met Mahmud, it was different because we were both in the WAY Foundation. We just hit it off.

It was strange being physical with someone new the first time. I had only ever had one partner. I had to get used to somebody new, but it just felt right. I did get emotional once. I actually thought I saw Ian. It was very, very strange. It really freaked me. I thought I saw Ian in Mahmud's face, even though Ian is white and Mahmud is Asian. I just opened my eyes and for a minute I saw Ian. I got emotional because, to me, it was Ian saying: 'It's fine.' It was as though he was giving me his blessing. I cried with relief.

I had no sense of guilt loving someone else; I wonder whether that is because it had been three and a half years since Ian died. I knew he would not want me to be on my own. His mum and his sister always said to me that I needed to move on and find someone else, that I was only young.

My relationship with Mahmud is different because I am not eighteen any more and there are the children. I always said to myself that if I did meet someone else, I would not introduce them to the children until I was absolutely certain. They got to know Mahmud as a friend at barbecues and picnics. It was a while before we told them that he was more than a friend. It did feel funny at thirty-nine years old to be telling my son that I had a *boyfriend*. At first, he was shocked and a bit upset. I explained to him: 'Daddy's gone and Mummy gets very lonely when you are in bed.' I decided not to go any further until he was happy. After a couple of days, Joshua asked to talk to me and said he was happy for Mahmud to be my boyfriend. He has been absolutely fine ever since and now wants to know whether we are going to marry. The baby, John, has never known a father figure and adores Mahmud, so it is a lot easier.

It just feels right between us. Mahmud is such a caring bloke. He gives me flowers every month. I am not used to it. Although I know Ian loved me, he was not one for things like that. Mahmud and I have both gone through the worst and we both deserve some happiness together.

My mum is a widow and she is in a relationship with a widower. She has always said that she couldn't love her new husband as she loves my dad. I could never love Mahmud the same as Ian. But I do love him very much, just differently. It is different because Ian was my first love and we had two children together. We had lived together for seventeen years and it would be impossible to say that I could love Mahmud in the same way. Mahmud will always love Sharon, but it is different for him because they were only together for five years. The chances are that *we* will be together for more than five years.

I do not feel the presence of his first wife, Sharon, although there are lots of her photographs that we have framed. I have helped him unpack her stuff into the new house. She is all around us and always will be, but I have never felt her presence. She will be part of our lives, just as Ian will. Mahmud talks about her, and I talk about him. Sharon is no threat to me, as Ian is not to Mahmud. If I had met a divorcee, there would always be the ex-wife there in the background. If Mahmud had not experienced widowhood himself, he would always be thinking that I am yearning my lost love and he would be threatened by this. Because we have both been through the same thing, we can both accept what has happened. To be honest, I think it is the perfect relationship to be in.

The hardest thing was telling my mother-in-law. I cried when I told her. It was not because I felt guilty but, being a mother myself, I could understand how she would feel. Ian was her baby. She was brilliant and said: 'You are young. Ian has gone and you have got to move on.' Everybody who cares for me has been brilliant. The only bad reaction I had was from my mum. It was not because I am in a relationship but because Mahmud is Asian. It is very sad. I told her it was something she had to accept because that is the way things are. I am not young any more and I make my own choices. Lately, she has accepted and he is now on her Christmas-present list, which is a huge step.

There have been comments about it being too soon. That was my biggest barrier in the beginning and why I didn't want to take it any further. I couldn't understand how Mahmud could be in a position to have a relationship so soon. For me, at that stage, it would never have crossed my mind. Because he has no children, he had a lot of time to grieve quickly, whereas I had children and could not get my head round it. I know that Mahmud still has bad days, but I know he is happy. It is sad when people make comments, because we are happy and we are sure. It is particularly so when other widowed people judge us. Everybody is different and there should not be any set guidelines for how quickly you have got to grieve and what stages you have to go through.

I think there is a difference between widows and widowers. They say that men remarry quickly. People do feel more sorry for men when they are bereaved, particularly when they have children. I did not get any help at all, except for a couple of weeks. I had to do it all myself. If I had been a crumbling wreck, I might have had more help.

I took off my wedding ring a couple of years after Ian died. People reacted as if I had done something wrong. I just said: 'Well, I am not married any more.' Perhaps I was beginning to feel that, if a man approached me, I might not want him to think I was married. I moved my engagement and eternity rings to my other hand. I know Mahmud still wears his and Sharon's on his wedding finger. I think it is just because he is used to wearing it. When he sees me, he takes it off. It does not bother me, if that is what he wants to do. At the WAY Foundation, there is a lot of discussion about when is the right time to take it off. There is no right time, I suppose. I have heard of people taking it off at the funeral because they don't feel married any more. It did not feel like a big step to me. I just took it off and put it in a box.

Once I said something slightly negative about Ian to a fellow widow. She said she was glad to hear me talking like that, as most people made out that their late partner was the bee's knees. Ian was not perfect; far from it, and neither am I. He was a wonderful man and I loved him to bits. Mahmud is the same. As much as he loved Sharon, he knew she had her faults, and we will talk about them and Ian's faults.

Ian will always be part of our lives because of the children. They are so like him. I showed them the video Ian made in South America. It makes this whole nightmare bearable as he looks so happy. In fact, I watched it with Mahmud. It was quite moving. It felt as if I was introducing him and saying: 'This is Ian and this is what he was like.' It was weird because I was looking at my first love on the screen and I was sitting cuddled up on the sofa with Mahmud.

We have had ups and downs. Mahmud is not used to having moody children around. Despite all this, we are getting married next year. We haven't told people because they'd probably think we're mad. When you have gone through what we've gone through, you learn that life is very precious. We both know how quickly it can end, as we both lost a partner so suddenly. Why wait, I suppose? He is a good man.

I feel that Ian would be happy for me. He would feel I have done my time. I will miss him for ever, but he is gone. He would be happy as long as who I chose is good to the children. They are the most important thing in my life.

I am not sure if I believe in God any more. I suppose it is because I am angry. Ian always said: 'When you're gone, you're gone.' Mahmud and I have laughed about what would happen if there was a heaven. Would it be all four of us together? Would we all swap stories? We both said, whichever one of us goes first, we know there will be someone there to meet us. We have also discussed the fact that if Mahmud and Ian are *both* in Heaven when I die, who will I go to?

Mahmud's story

Mahmud is a widower with no children. Two months after losing his wife, he met Kerri, a widow with two children.

Six months ago, I lost my wife, Sharon, when she was only thirty-two. I was thirty-four. It isn't the sort of thing you even contemplate happening.

She got up to go to work, feeling fine, and she collapsed in the shower. She had had a brain haemorrhage. I thought she had just fainted. I tried to revive her and called an ambulance. I couldn't feel a heartbeat. They took her into hospital but they did not tell me that her heart and lungs had already stopped at home. It was surreal. It was like being in a nightmare. One of the sisters put her arms round me, saying how she had been widowed at the age of twenty-five and knew how I was feeling. That meant an awful lot to me. I did not feel as alone and unique as you can do in these situations.

Sharon wanted to be an organ donor, so they needed to keep her body warm. She had been taken into intensive care for this to happen even though she was already dead. Staying overnight in the hospital was the most horrendous experience. They did the brainstem testing and then it was all over. The hardest thing I had to do was to walk away from her in the hospital. I tried it three times before I could do it.

After her organs had been removed, I saw her in the chapel of rest. It was the first person I had known who had died. It was truly shocking, because she had gone from warm and pink to cold and white. I kissed her lips, which was a chilling experience. Later, the surgeon told me that her organs had saved four people. I was crying my eyes out but laughing at the same time.

We had only been married eighteen months and, in fact, our second wedding anniversary will be next Tuesday. Between Sharon dying and the funeral, I couldn't sleep, so I got on the Internet and typed in 'widow' and 'young'. It came up with the WAY Foundation. That has been the most important thing for me.

I spoke at the funeral, which was ten days after she died. That was very difficult. As a Muslim, it was hard to cremate her, but she had happened to mention she wanted it. For me, it meant we could not be buried together when I died. We had the reception back in the place we got married.

My family live in London and I am in Leeds, but I was quite pleased to have the distance. I would have found it claustrophobic. I wanted to grieve at my own speed and not have people fussing over me. The thought of living another fifty years without her was extremely scary. The initial thought is that you want to die, although I was never suicidal.

You do not want to kill yourself, but you do want to die. You are not afraid of death.

The WAY Foundation helped by allowing me to talk to other people like me. It's just a collection of people like me, but it helps on a number of levels. You are able to talk to someone who has been through the same things and you know that what you feel is not unique. You do not get treated with pity, which is what you get from your friends and family. You can be normal. What makes you special also makes *them* special. Therefore, you are *not* special. It has helped me get over the question: 'Why me?' I also had counselling. I didn't use it so much to help me grieve but more for life decisions, for example, whether to go ahead with our new house.

I was lucky – maybe that is the wrong word – that I did not have children. This gave me the time to grieve because I could just think about myself. We would have had children. We had pregnancy books around. When I lost Sharon, I lost the children we were going to have as well. I felt as if my whole life, my whole future, every plan we had made, had been shattered. We were so young, so we had never thought about wills or anything.

At the time of Sharon's death, we were living with my mother-in-law, as we were waiting for our new house to be ready. After she died, ninety-nine per cent of the time it was good being together. But I felt she had her own grief and issues. I felt like sometimes there was a bit of a competition of grief. Recently, I moved into the new house Sharon and I had been planning. She had dreamt non-stop about what she was going to do here. I felt it was important for her that I moved in. As she had never been in the house except as a shell, I don't remember her at every corner. We had chosen everything together. To have walked away from it would have been harder. I do feel that this is where she would want me to be.

However, I do not feel she has been around me since she died. I know a lot of people feel that they can talk to their lost ones, but I don't. When I go to the crematorium, I talk to her there. I do believe she is in Heaven and hope she is content. She was tired, like we all are. She was a real angel.

I genuinely believe that she would want me to be happy. When I was in hospital with her, I was praying that I could switch places with her. But now I am glad it was her that went and not me. To think of her pining and in agony as I have been would break my heart. I asked myself, if she were in my position and found someone so soon, how would I feel? Would I not get upset? The human part of me says that I would be upset, but there is no going back. I would want her to be content and you cannot have it both ways. I feel it is alright to be happy with someone new and still cherish the memory of what I had. My wife will always be part of who I am and will always be in my heart.

I met Kerri at a dinner two months after Sharon died. We got on like a house on fire and became the best of friends. It turned out we worked in the same company. A couple of months later, we got together. We wanted to take it slowly. Although it could have been confusing moving on to a romantic level, it wasn't. It felt separate. I have never compared her to my wife. They are very different. My wife was very independent, whereas Kerri and I do many things together. I do not have those moments when I say 'I remember doing this with my wife.' However, they are similar in the way they both take the mickey out of me, mercilessly.

As we are both widowed, I don't feel the need to pretend that I didn't have a wife or shouldn't talk about her. We both have someone else. I have heard other widowed people with partners who are not widowed say how difficult it is to be open. There are all sorts of issues, like the non-widowed partner worrying about whether they are just a crutch, how far should they support the one who is grieving. Even though Kerri and I both have the same issues, it is still difficult to get the balance right. Kerri needs to feel she is as important to me as my wife.

One of the best things about being with someone who is widowed means that there are four people in our relationship. We both accept this and are very supportive of it in each other. I know some people have been banned from having photos and things like that. In my case, my love for Sharon and Kerri is different. My love for Sharon will always be there. It is in a compartment all on its own. The love I feel for Kerri is in a different compartment. I know many widowed people who are not ready for a relationship because they are not in that place yet.

Even though I felt ready, in the early days, it was Kerri who had trouble with our relationship starting so soon after Sharon's death. She also worried about what other people would say. It is an eye-opener for me that people do not respect the feeling between two people. They judge it according to some preconceived idea. Just as there is no set time for when you should be 'over it', there is no set time for when you should be in a relationship. Everybody is different. It is surprising that those who do the judging are not only those who haven't been bereaved but also those who are widowed. Especially those with children. I think that this is because when you have children, you don't have time for yourself, and the grieving process is slower. You can't grieve when you need to, only when the children allow you to. This makes it harder to understand how anyone could move on faster than yourself. They use where they were, say at six months, as a benchmark and expect others to be at the same point. If you are further ahead than they were at this time, they will say: 'I'm worried about you because when I was [at] six months, I had a break-down.' Their judgement point is a very personal one. I know that I am a lot further on in my grief than they are.

I had the time to read every book I could get my hands on. I have done so much reading, so much counselling and so much thinking that I have got to the place that everything I had with Sharon is in my heart. I now can have something new with someone else without feeling a conflict.

At the WAY Foundation, we do talk about relationships but also about practical things, like: When do you take your wedding ring off? What do you say to your children? When do you start meeting people? You do share a very intimate bond because you share a very raw and personal experience. That is what Kerri and I have together. You are drawn to people that have experienced the same thing. If things go wrong, there is a danger of blaming it on your bereavement, but some relationships just do not work.

There is a lot of banter and a lot of theory about how men seem to marry again much faster than widows. A lot of women think that men cannot cope on their own. Another theory is that men do not have the kind of friendships in which they can offload their feelings and, there-fore, they find they only get this in a new relationship.

Everyone knows about our relationship, apart from my mother-in-law. Even though she has suggested that I should go and find someone, it is one thing saying it and another thing reacting to it. Why should I put her through all that? My family were concerned that it was too soon. They were also concerned with my taking on Kerri's two children. I have met Kerri's mother-in-law. It is hard for her, whether she is saying it or not, because she has lost her son. For Kerri, it's been three and a half years, so everyone would think enough time had passed for her to start a new relationship. I feel with Sharon's mother there is this social thing that it isn't decent to have a relationship for a certain length of time afterwards. It is a strong taboo, but there is no sense to it.

Everyone on Kerri's side is happy for her, and my friends are over the moon. My family and friends who live further away find it hard because they are grieving at a different rate to me. I lived my grief every day; they would only be grieving when they speak to me. They stopped instantly they put down the phone. Their grief is five minutes here, five minutes there. I am moving faster than them. I think one of the main issues with this taboo is that other people have not moved on. It is more of a shock to them.

Kerri and I have talked a lot about the future. It cannot be overestimated how hard it is to plan for the future when you have had all your plans taken away from you. The thought of what tomorrow holds, what the years ahead hold, is completely shocking. But we have been doing this and it's good. I am completely there. Everything feels just right, but it is hard to communicate that to other people. So as not to upset people, we sometimes feel we have to behave differently in public to how we do in private. This will get better because we are planning to get engaged and hope to get married next summer on Kerri's fortieth birthday.

Obviously I would give anything to be back where I was. But that is not an option and it's a wasted emotion. I have never had anyone to blame and I am happy with those five years of my life. What is strange, and even terrifying, is the thought that if it does work with Kerri, I will have a relationship which lasts far in excess of what I had with Sharon. The person you have lost means the world to you, and it is scary to think of having a relationship with someone else that will outlast that and will potentially be better as a result. You fear that it somehow diminishes all that passion and emotion that you had in the first relationship. You have said goodbye to someone who was the most important person in the whole world to you, and they will always be important. However, the new person will become *as* important, if not *more* important. It is really hard to come to terms with that.

Kerri, having been widowed longer, has had time to form a separate identity from her husband. The Kerri who was married is a very different person to the one she was four and a half years ago. I am not the same person that I was when my wife was here. I have been changed by the bereavement. I suspect you change even more in time.

I have never felt threatened knowing that Kerri loved someone else. Her husband will always be her children's father. I do not want to change their identity by making them take my name. I will support Kerri in any way she wants to remember and honour her husband's memory. For my second wedding anniversary next week, I will be going to the crematorium. I will take the day off work and I might try to sort out some of her stuff. I have not really done that. Some bits of my grief are done but other bits... I wanted to unpack all of my wife's stuff into the new house. It would have meant a lot to her to have her clothes hanging up. I suspect if Kerri had not come along, Sharon's clothes would be hanging up in my wardrobe. I have not done this, as I did not think it would be right, because I have moved on a little bit to someone else. There is a little room with Sharon's things in it. On our first wedding anniversary we went back to the place where we were married. I might go back this year. Our wedding felt like yesterday, to be honest.

I have been to Hell and back. I cannot stress how much the WAY Foundation has helped. You realise how amazing people are, and it humbles you. A lot of people come from far more tragic situations than yourself and they do not even realise how awful it is because they are surviving. They say death teaches you not about death but about living, and that is the secret to all this, once you realise that grief is not about the death but how you react to it. It is important to deal with my grief in a way that my wife would be proud of.

Elizabeth's story

Elizabeth is a widowed psychotherapist in her sixties.

As a psychotherapist, I come into contact with many people with different experiences of death. I feel although I am familiar with aspects of the grieving process, I have not yet recovered from my own bereavements.

Three years ago, my husband died of an asthma attack, and within a few months my mother died. It is still very early days. I really believe in the continuing of bonds after death as opposed to the grief work theory. By this, I mean that I believe that I will continue to have a relationship with my husband after his death as opposed to the idea that I will grieve through the different stages and then finish with it. We may have been parted in death but not in love. Therefore, why should my relationship with my husband stop just because it is not on a physical level? With that in mind, I feel personally that divorce is far more painful.

I could not possibly enter into a relationship with anyone else yet. I know, however, that if I had died, my husband would be in a relationship by now. Men are different. In fact, my elderly father commenced a relationship with the nurse at seventy-nine years old, while my mother was dying.

I feel this behaviour is all about the Oedipal aspects of life. Men will always seek out a surrogate mother. This is purely my opinion. This does not mean, however, that men need a female for their sense of identity. I think what actually happens is that women are often swamped by the male, and they are the ones who relinquish their identity. Perhaps this has changed a little amongst younger women. I also feel that women are more bonded in any relationship than men. Men do not seem to form that depth of bond.

I was asked recently by a researcher for contacts with anybody who had been widowed and was now involved in new relationships. I had to say I did not know any *women* who had moved on. All the women I know were still grieving. I feel this is not unexpected. Women grieve slowly and would be confused dealing with both grief and a new relationship. I personally think that if people form a new relationship too soon, it does not bode well for the future. I also fear for the children, who have to adapt to seeing their parent in a new relationship before they have grieved.

I know that many bereavement counsellors would have different opinions on this subject, but this is my own conclusion.

෪

Richard's story

Richard is a young widower with two small children. After a few false starts, he has settled into a new relationship.

My wife, Mary, was diagnosed with breast cancer on the day of my youngest child's second birthday. She had a year of intensive treatment to try and cure it, mastectomy, chemotherapy and radiotherapy, followed by nine horrendous months of being terminally ill. During this time, she became progressively more of an invalid. Finally, as it went to her brain, she was not really there at all.

We had plenty of time to discuss stuff and make arrangements, which was very good, as I feel that she left everything well planned and organised for me. However, nothing did prepare me for being left totally alone with two kids, even though I had been a modern father. I remember shortly after she died being in a swimming pool with one going one way and the other going the other way, thinking: 'Now what? Which one do I go after?'

I got lots of support from my church and work, and the NHS was excellent. Local people and friends were very good. All family on both sides were absolutely useless and so they are out of my will!

I have been to bereavement meetings. I just wanted to shoot the breeze and talk about a way forward. The women there just wanted to go over and over what they had been through, often many years after the event. I think there is a difference there between men and women. Eighteen months after my wife died, I feel I have moved on. I do know some widows who have moved on in a similar timescale. I was told that, as a widower with young children, I would be attractive to women. That hasn't been the case. It doesn't surprise me. Why should women be attracted to me when there are loads of blokes out there who don't have to look after their kids and can move in without any ties? However, since I have had a girlfriend, I have had women throwing themselves at me. But that's another story.

Starting a new relationship has been interesting. There were lots of false starts – hopefully not too much damage done to others. It took me quite a while to work out what I was looking for and why I was looking for it. It turned out that what I wanted was a girlfriend–boyfriend type of relationship, mainly focused on going out and doing things together (cinema, meals, country houses, city breaks, rock shows), rather than a little 'wifey' to iron the clothes and cook for the children. It took me a bit of time to work that out. Then, when I was dating, although the girls said that was what they wanted, usually they were looking for the man who had left them.

At first, it felt strange to be having a physical relationship with someone new. I don't know whether the speed at which you move on is about the difference between the sexes but, in my experience, the difference is more to do with the types of death that people have experienced. Where cancer is involved and the partner has been very ill, operated on, pumped full of noxious chemicals and irradiated to look like a week spent on a beach without sun cream, then there isn't much intimacy. This means, in my experience, that those left behind are keen for sex. Where the death is a sudden one and there has been a normal relationship beforehand, then intimacy is not such a big issue.

My wife is still very present. So much so that I feel she is there to confirm and justify anything I do *with* her. And, of course, she is the little boys' mother. I have given up work to bring them up for a few years. They are seven and five now. We feel her presence, and she is pretty deeply embedded in our day-to-day lives.

My friends have been happy to see me move on. I haven't told any of my family or Mary's family, as I think it would be difficult for them. I know my family think there is a timescale in which it would be decent. I don't know what their timescale is. It's probably the rest of my life, so I haven't worried them with it!

My children have adjusted fairly well to my new relationship. The youngest was fine but the eldest one had some teething problems. We have taken it very slowly. My girlfriend doesn't live with us, so it is predominantly about going out together.

I don't think I glorify Mary's memory, not really, not at all. I do keep with me some elements of my wife's character that I think were exceptional and are lessons for me. For example, she was incredibly brave to know she was going to die and leave her young children. Yet, she never complained. This made it a lot easier for me to bear.

My girlfriend accepts the reality of my wife. I think, though, that she finds it threatening that I still love her.

At the end of the day, I hope my death will be painless and short. I am not expecting to be confronted by my wife and have to go through a list of complaints as to what I did and did not do!

Gwyneth's story

Gwyneth's husband committed suicide, leaving her with one child. She is currently in an unsettled relationship.

My husband, Gareth, died two years ago after ten years of marriage. It was not completely out of the blue. I had sent him to the doctor three months before because he was in a very low mood, crying silently, tears streaming down his face. He had a history of mental illness. We had not been married long before our daughter, Alice, was born. We were both social workers.

There was a lot of bizarre behaviour all the time. The doctor referred him to a psychiatric hospital, but he killed himself before he got the appointment. There was a lot of guilt when he finally did it. During the last few weeks, his behaviour was irrational and he started to become violent. The child-protection people said I should put an injunction on him for my daughter's sake. I got the power of arrest against him on the Friday and he killed himself on the Monday. My daughter was seven at the time.

He hanged himself. I still can't believe that he hanged himself in the hallway of the home of his eighty-three-year-old mother, who he loved. I am totally surprised he did that to his mum. You cannot get your head around it.

There is no sense of relief. I loved him. I didn't love his illness. If you live with mental illness, you can't just say he's 'a bit of a bastard'. When he finally did it, I was grief-stricken. I wanted to explain to him what I was doing and why I had taken out the injunction. We could have sorted it out. I never got the chance to explain it all to him. Unfinished business is difficult.

I loved him through it all. It makes it difficult for me to form another relationship. My daughter made a poster a couple of days after he died advertising for a new daddy. The first year was a roller-coaster. It is too big. You can't look at it head-on. There is no part of you that is separate from it, no part that can be objective. There is nothing you can do to help you come through it. You just have to hang on in there, really. If you get through, you do.

Quite soon after he died, I thought about moving on. I think I was quite pragmatic about it. I have no family, a sister I never see, my father is a stroke victim. Alice wanted me to get a new daddy so I went to a dating agency, where I met David. He is from the Valleys. Welsh Valleys culture is very family-orientated and they are old-fashioned and dutiful. He was an ex-miner who had raised six children to adulthood. His wife had left him and he wanted a new family. We got on alright in the beginning. But quite soon, there were problems, because he was jealous of Gareth, my husband. I still hadn't got over him. If I ever talked about him, David did not like it. *I* didn't like it that *he* didn't like it. He would say: 'That's in the past now.' But it isn't in the past. It is a life-changing experience, something that changes you for ever. Saying you've got to get over it and move on is to misunderstand the enormity of it. It trivialises it. I felt he really doesn't know me at all. Despite this, David still wants to marry me. He even has got my name and Alice's tattooed on his arm.

Alice calls him 'Daddy'. She asked him to be her daddy right from the first. Alice is remarkable. She still says: 'I miss my dad', but it's always with a fondness, not neediness. I have tried my best to protect her. She is one of the reasons why David and I are together. Even when we fall out, they want to see each other. She does need to call somebody 'Daddy' for some odd reason. She knows he is not her father.

I probably loved David in the beginning. It was a relief having him around. He was so good to me as well. He redecorated the whole house and he really looked after me. He still does. But it is an on-and-off relationship. Sometimes we don't see each other for a couple of weeks, but it's still on.

Being physical with someone new was not difficult, but it was the emotional stuff that really was. I miss so much about my husband Gareth. He was very intelligent, very talented, a brilliant musician. People used to say: 'You are joined at the hip, you two.' That aspect of being absolutely known is lacking. You can't replace it. Maybe you settle for less if you don't know there is more. David says: 'I feel second-best. I can't compete with a dead man.' When we have arguments, he says: 'You are still in love with your dead husband.' And it is all true.

I have still got all his things around: photos, even his broken guitar. I couldn't move the book he was reading at the time in case it upset him. It took ages to get rid of his clothes. I needed wardrobe space but got rid of my stuff, not his.

Because of the nature of how he died, there was a lot of silence from people. Nobody has ever mentioned it since. Even his boss and wife, whose children are at the same school as Alice, have never mentioned Gareth at all. No one phoned up and asked how we were doing. It's a weird one. Maybe they feel they could have made more of an effort and there is a lot of guilt. His family won't have anything to do with me since he died. Alice has lost the whole extended family. They banned me from the funeral because of the injunction. Alice and I held our own memorial.

David, my new man, is much easier to live with. He would be hard-pushed to better Gareth. It is strange coming to terms with life being less turbulent. David is very good with Alice. You have to be careful when you are widowed. You are very vulnerable. I knew I had to find somebody trustworthy with children and make sure that somebody wasn't after my money. My gran said: 'You have got to be careful who you hook up with now.'

I don't know why David wants to stay with me. He says he loves me, but we're totally different. He works shifts and he does not read and write. Although we get on all right, there is a huge intellectual gulf. I don't feel I am waiting for someone better to come along. At forty-four, I'm getting a bit old for it all. I feel ancient and lived-out. I don't know whether I am capable of having somebody else or whether I can let myself be hurt any more. I don't think I would ever get close to anyone again.

§

Belinda's story

Belinda was widowed when her husband died suddenly. They had no children. She later married Tony, a friend of her husband's, and went on to have two children.

I was widowed three days after my thirty-sixth birthday. I had been married to Roy for thirteen years, when he died suddenly of a heart attack, aged thirty-eight. We had both been aware for many years that he had heart disease, but there was no indication that his health had deteriorated to the levels his post-mortem revealed.

Roy had always said that I should '…give it six months to make it look decent then go and find someone else'! Whilst I had never seriously intended to follow this advice, not long after Roy's death, I found myself forming a relationship with Tony, a chap whom Roy and I had known for some time.

Tony was still married when we first met, but the relationship was over. His first wife was already seeing, and is now married to, his ex-'best friend'. Looking back, we probably were drawn together as we each provided the other with an emotional crutch and big shoulders for crying on.

Neither of us had children from our first marriages, but a year later our son, Jack, was born. Tony and I married. Three years after that, our daughter, Niamh, completed the family.

Thankfully, my children haven't had to cope with losing a parent because I lost Roy before they were born. However, they have had to deal with Mummy crying for no obvious reason, and suffered the fall-out from the depressions that hit me from time to time. They have been brought up knowing all about Roy and consider him a part of their family.

Even though Roy made it clear that I should find someone else, I had not planned on moving on. It was very natural, not a considered decision. Sometimes, I think I did not have enough time to grieve properly. It probably hit me about two years later when Jack was born. It is not necessarily wrong to move on quickly. I had a friend whose mother died. Her father had taken care of her to the last. One month later, her father moved his girlfriend in. They are still together now, eighteen years later. However, I have to find grieving time within this, my new, family. For some people, the grieving will go on for ever. It's different for everyone. In my experience, there are no rules. The only people who tell you how long you should grieve before moving on are those who have not been through it.

Tony moved in with me. The house has gradually changed. He moved in mainly because I could not bear to leave the house. It was so much Roy. When Tony and I looked like we were going to be long-term, I realised it had to become *his* home too. The bricks and mortar are still the same, but there is very little resemblance to the old house.

The photos of Roy and me in the hallway came down naturally because of decorating. Other bits and pieces of his are still very much in evidence in the house. I dealt with his clothes early on, which was really hard. I have kept a special T-shirt of his and a wide trilby hat and jacket he liked. They sit on our coat peg. Roy is in evidence. It was his home and it still is. It is Tony's home and the children's home too.

Who wants to remember the bad times? There is no fun in having unhappy memories. I sometimes tend to forget the bad bits, but I know that Roy could be a moody beggar. I have to struggle to remember that part, but it is necessary. If you do start to glorify the dead, then the living can't compare. I don't compare my two husbands. Tony is completely different from Roy. There is no comparison, physically or in personality. Tony has no problem with me loving Roy. I asked him if he was jealous. I think he is but he said: 'No, how can I be jealous of someone who does not exist any more? You're not going to go off and leave me for him.' It helps that he knew Roy. The day before he died, they had packed their bags to go off working together. It took a while to get over that one.

My son Jack understands that Roy was my first husband. I had decided I would keep Roy's surname Farmer, even though I was marrying Tony. For the first few days of his life in the hospital, he was known as 'Baby Farmer'. I had an odd minute a month ago when he said to someone: 'Tony is my second dad. Roy was my first dad.' Part of me was actually quite chuffed, because Roy would have been chuffed to have been a dad. My daughter is that bit younger. She understands that Roy lives with God. She asked the other day if she could go and visit him. They describe him as their 'friend'. We have always talked about Roy, because we wanted to avoid awkward questions later.

Roy's mother was happy for me. She's dead now. She knew that Roy and I had wanted kids. She was quite aware that time would run out for me if I did not get on with it. We all still exchange Christmas cards with his family. They live close by, and we get invited to family functions. At Roy's mum's eightieth, we were the only people who weren't direct family. I felt very proud to be included in that one.

I still miss Roy every day of my life. Building a life with Tony has been hard work. It is a hell of a thing to deal with and unbelievably emotional. If it happens to you, you suddenly realise how strong humans can be. The joys and tribulations of parenting have helped me to move forward and be positive about the future. I feel I have been very, very lucky. Roy was a wonderful husband. I feel immensely proud and grateful to have been able to share his life. We travelled together on our motorbikes and had wonderful life experiences. What we missed was having a family. With Tony, I have everything I did not have with Roy. I have to think that way, or else it can feel too tragic.

Tony's story

Tony is married to Belinda, the widow of his friend. They have two children. They are both in their thirties.

Roy and I used to meet up in the pub and play darts. We had lads' nights out. It was a shock when he died. We were supposed to go out to Greece to do some building work together, but he died just a few days before. He was thirty-eight. I was thirty.

At that time, I was splitting up with my wife, who went off with one of my best friends from school. Sometimes, I think it is hard because I know she is still around and about. All of us went to Roy's funeral on motorbikes. I knew Belinda, because she used to work in the pub on a Wednesday night. Neither of us had children.

Very soon after Roy died, we just got talking at one of the motorbike shows and it just carried on from there. We talked about my wife and me splitting up and Roy's death. We were both really upset, and we had a lot in common. Over the next few weeks, we started seeing each other. We did not tell anybody, because we were a little bit embarrassed about what people might think. Roy had not been dead that long and I had only just split. We told good friends, like Robert, early and he said it was all alright. Roy had said for Robert to watch over her. Roy's brother is a biker too, and we get on really well. He was happy for Belinda. Roy came from a really big family, who were all really happy too.

Belinda and me being together felt awkward – not embarrassing, but awkward. We didn't know what they were going to say. Some people agree with it, some don't. It doesn't matter, but we did keep it secret. The people who needed to know knew about it.

We did get together quite soon after Roy died, but we comforted each other. It was funny being with a friend's wife. You think: 'Should I be here or shouldn't I?' I think you get used to that. There's nothing anyone can do about it. He'd be happy about us being together.

Roy always knew he would die one day because he had had a stroke a few years earlier, but not when. He carried on life as if nothing was the matter. There was not a lot he could do about it. Sometimes, I think Roy is around. Sometimes, he could possibly be there watching.

I don't compare myself with him. We don't look the same. He had a big bushy beard and a beer belly. I'm the same height, but a bit slimmer. He was a great character, a good laugh. He knew what was wrong but used to make light of it, especially in front of people like us.

I moved into Belinda and Roy's house. I contribute to the mortgage, so it's my home as well now. I've changed things around. I'm a builder, so I just go ahead and do things. I have made my mark on it. The rooms have been decorated, but it is still the same house. The photographs are still up, not all of them. We have got some of Roy and Belinda, some of me and Belinda, and some of all of us all up on the same shelf. It doesn't bother me. All our friends are up there too. I suppose the photographs will still be up wherever we go.

Sometimes, I feel Belinda is still thinking about Roy. We talk about him but not as much as we used to. We went to Greece to stay with the friends that Roy was supposed to work with before he died. That was really difficult for Belinda to do. When we went out for a meal one night, his friend called me Roy. He had known Belinda and Roy much longer. In fact, he was one of his best friends. He just forgot. He said: 'I'm sorry.' I didn't mind. We had a good laugh about it.

Roy's ashes are scattered in Roy's best friend Robert's field, under a tree. Belinda and me want to be scattered there together as well. We still see Robert, because he is godfather to one of our children.

Sometimes I believe in Heaven, sometimes I don't know. I should hope that we'll all meet up. In fact, we'll all have a big party, because since Roy went, we have lost six or seven people from the pub. At this rate, we will all be up there soon. It is very peculiar, because we only live in a little village of about a hundred.

Our children are now seven and four. Jack, the first one, was born fifteen months after Roy died and Niamh, my daughter, three years later. Looking back, some of it has been difficult. It's best if you can talk about things and get it out of the way. The trickiest bit has been my divorce. I haven't seen my ex since she went off. It's taken a while, but I have got over it. The first year or so was a bit awkward because I didn't know whether I could trust people or not. I get nervous if Belinda is away. She is still grieving and getting over her husband. It's a bit of a job to deal with it all. I think Belinda still loves him. That's OK. It helps having known him.

Fatma's story

Fatma is a Sunni Muslim who was widowed after her husband was killed in Somalia. They had two children. She is now remarried and has just had a new baby.

In 1995, there was a civil war in Somalia and my husband was killed. My baby was four months old and my son was two years old. We were living with my husband and father. My mother had already left for Nairobi because she was frightened of the situation, but my husband did not want to leave. A lot of our tribe didn't leave, and then they were massively slaughtered. It was a lost cause. You have to accept death. My religion says it has to be tolerated. If not, my head would have become crazy. When my husband died, I did not have time to grieve. There was just survival.

Many people had to stay or they were frightened to leave. They cut our water off. We had no contact with the outside. I managed eventually to contact my mother by telegraph. I gave her name and tribe and described her. They found her in Nairobi, and she sent me money to escape.

I stayed in Nairobi for nine months. I was living illegally with no passport, and I had to hide. The police were very strong there. Then I moved to Tanzania and lived there for years, where it was easier to hide. In 1999, I came to England. I had to live in hostels with my children. They were terrible places, sharing rooms and everything. Then they gave me a small flat.

How did I cope with the grief? I suppose I used my religion. It has given me structure. In my religion, which is Sunni Muslim, if a woman's husband has died, she is expected to grieve for four months and four days. A husband grieves for just three days. This is because although men are strong physically, they have their needs. You are not allowed to scream or cry out loud. You can cry lots of tears from your heart, but you have to control yourself. What can we do about death? We can't stop it as it is part of life. For four months and four days, we are not allowed to wear any new clothes – nothing bright, no henna, nothing attractive, no make-up. We can bathe, carry out ablutions and we pray. After this time, we can marry.

In my brain, I did not want to remarry. I have to look after my two children. They are the most important things to me. I felt that a man might not be caring for my children. I was absolutely adamant about not marrying. Everyone kept asking me and presenting me with men, but I did not want to know. We are not allowed to have boyfriends but, anyway, I was not interested. It was not my plan. In the Koran, no one is allowed to force women to get married, although the culture has corrupted that.

When I got married, all my family were shocked. I was happy with my children. I had a girl and a boy. I did not need to marry. Many men were interested, but I always said no. Then I met my new husband, who is a distant relative. God struck. It was beyond my control.

How does it feel to love someone else? Women always think that their first is special. All my friends say to me that their first husband is the one. When someone dies, you remember the good. With divorce, you remember the bad. My present husband jokes with me and laughs, saying: 'Why is he better than me?' But I do feel that. I can't help remembering him as the very special one. In my religion, it is the way to be offered to your brother-in-law if your husband dies. But you can choose to say no. Brothers often joke that they do not want to marry their sisters-in-law in case they will say: 'My brother was better than you', because they know they love the first ones best. They don't want to feel jealous and have bad thoughts about their dead brother.

Historically, in Somalia, if the widow refuses to marry her brother-in-law when her husband dies, her father-in-law would take the children and the money, everything. Many women refused to marry their brother-in-law, even under this threat. Somali women are very strong. Our culture is more moderate now.

Men are still allowed four wives. If they lose one of them, they will feel the loss as keenly as if they were the only one.

My dead husband is present in my life now. I pray to him every day. My children pray to him and give words to him. If I was able to go to Mecca and Hajj, I would like to offer prayers for him. My second husband knows this. I would not have married him if he did not allow me or my children to think of their dead father. I still have to respect my first husband's family, and I send them presents. My husband asks me who I would like to be with in Heaven. I just laugh at this. There is the story of the Prophet. He had nine wives and they asked this question about Heaven, and the Prophet said: 'It is up to the wives to decide.'

My new husband is much older than I am. I am thirty-five. He is very experienced. I chose him because he is good to my children. A younger man might just want *me* and not my children. I am older now and love is different. I really do love my first husband and I still miss him. I do not feel bad about this. It is just a fact. It was completely normal to remarry. I think it is more abnormal not to want to.

I feel that I have accepted my new life. I am strong and I feel like nothing is new. I have had so many experiences and faced them. Death is part of life. We follow each other step by step until we go.

ᢍ

Lucia's story

Lucia is a widow in a new relationship. She is in her forties and has a teenage daughter.

My husband, Frankie, died of cancer two years ago after twenty years of marriage. He had been in remission but then, suddenly, it was back and he had six weeks to live. Our daughter, Sophie, was eleven at the time. She had to be very strong because she really was a daddy's girl. They lived for one another. We all lived for one another.

My marriage was fantastic and I miss everything about it. Frankie was my friend and my soulmate and we were going to be together for ever. Neither of us would ever have thought of straying. We had grown into one another and taken on each other's views on life. After twenty years, you do become one person. We were a great team and my loss is so immense.

I knew that I didn't want to be on my own. I had loved being part of a couple and was meant to be a wife and mother. That was my role and I was happy with that. I was never going to be a career girl. Eighteen months after Frankie died, I met Gary at the races. He is very different from my husband in many ways and I know, in my heart, that there is no future in it. I was not particularly interested in him at first, but when he pursued me, I was flattered. I felt some alarm bells going off, however, because he was recently separated and it hadn't been a clean break. Here we are six months down the line, and I am still seeing him.

But there is so much going on. My husband Frankie is the one I really want. At times, I have felt that I have taken two steps forward and three steps back and I wish I hadn't met Gary. I had got myself onto an even keel after the initial shock. I was doing well. Now, my life has huge ups and downs. Gary affects my moods. He doesn't understand what I'm going through. He claims to, but he is basically a selfish person. He has only experienced the death of his grandparents, and he doesn't really know the physical pain of grief.

My husband made me feel like a princess. I felt attractive and totally cherished, and that is so good for your confidence. I feel this chap is a stepping stone. I know he is also probably using *me* to a certain extent too. Gary is good for my self-esteem. There is this excitement when I am getting ready to go out with him and I feel twenty again. That's it, really. It acts as a distraction from the awfulness of it all. Although I feel I know the score about this, whenever I feel our relationship is coming to an end, I feel down. It is an adrenaline thing. It's confusing. I think what has happened is that I have become obsessed with Gary. A little part of me does love him, but maybe it's because he is attentive and says the nicest things.

I think my husband would disapprove of him. It's not that he would mind me moving on to a new person although, as he was dying, it wasn't something we talked about because that would have broken his heart. All he kept saying was: 'I want you to be happy.' He would not like Gary because of his lifestyle and because he is unreliable. Gary is everything that Frankie was not.

It is confusing, but I am driven to Gary. After Frankie died, I so missed being hugged. Not so much the sex, more the affection. My daughter, Sophie, used to sleep in my bed with me for a long time after. She is still in my room, although she has rejected me emotionally. She is fourteen and she really minds about the new chap. She doesn't want to know. I have said to her: 'This is how it is.' There have been lots and lots of tears. She doesn't want him in the house. Although she went for counselling immediately after Frankie died, now she doesn't want to talk to me about anything to do with Frankie's death and has clammed right up. The one thing she will say is that, no matter who it is, she doesn't want me to be with anyone. She has certainly not dealt with things. I can't imagine what she has gone through, and I know my own dad was pivotal to me. I try to talk to her sometimes, but she goes mental at me. She has gone from being my lovely girl to being this horrible… I cannot tell what is grief and what is teenage behaviour.

I cannot bear to take off my wedding ring, and I still have all of Frankie's clothes hanging in the wardrobe. I did think about putting them in boxes, but Sophie wasn't happy when I mentioned it. Frankie is still very much with me, but in some ways it is my family who won't let him go at all. They feel he is still my husband. They loved him, and they don't want me to have a new relationship. They certainly don't want to know about Gary and all got very huffy when they found out about us. My sister, who I am very close to, feels it's too soon. But I feel it's too soon for *her*. I know *my* needs. I felt I had to justify myself to her. When I said: 'This is ridiculous. I am forty and I don't feel as if I have a life of my own', she said that my daughter should be my life. But how can I be doing her justice if I am miserable? You would think she would want me to be happy. This has all upset me so much. When I suggested meeting Gary, my sister made it clear that her husband would not welcome him in their house. She has said she would approve if I found a 'nice widower' who is in the same situation as myself. She is worried that widows can be preyed upon and that Gary is after my money. As horrible as Gary is, that's not on his agenda. They also can't understand what he would see in me, because he is so much younger than me. Don't they think I am intelligent and know what I am doing?

Although I don't agree with my sister, I did wonder about a widower. I went to a dinner set up especially for widows and widowers. I started to talk to a man who seemed quite fun. We had a lot in common, losing our partners, our children's reactions, and so on. After a while, I realised that all he did was talk about how awful his situation was and how depressed he was. He was still obviously so deep in his bereavement, I felt I couldn't cope. I was in trouble enough with my own grief and I felt I would drown in his. I felt awful and guilty for feeling this way. This made me realise why I was with Gary: I want to be with people who can make me laugh. He has taken me away from misery. I feel I am entitled to enjoy myself. I want to live.

It is strange going to bed with someone new. You are confronted with this very different body from the one you are used to. Gary says he doesn't feel threatened that I still love my husband, but he always rushes out of our house when Sophie comes in. He says: 'It's your family home. It's your husband's house.' I have told him it was a wonderful marriage. He is worried that I am trying to replace Frankie and jumping ahead too quickly. I know I am not, because he does not even compare with Frankie.

I think I did put Frankie on a pedestal, but the truth is he did have faults. He had to go to Gamblers Anonymous, for instance. But family have got him as perfect in their minds and no one can live up to him. His own family, who had previously paid him no attention in his life, went into overdrive when he was in hospital. They bombarded us. We found this difficult. OK, it was his mother, but this sudden change was difficult.

After his death, there has been virtually nothing. I ring his mum out of duty, but I haven't seen them for a year. The sad thing is that Sophie has lost her cousins, who would have been a link to her dead father.

When Sophie is being difficult about Gary, I have tried to point out to her that her friends with divorced parents have to accept a new dad. She says: 'But their dad is still alive. I just want to hold my daddy.' I reply: 'I want to hold your daddy too.' She insists I'm still married to Frankie and that friends should be enough for me. But friends are not a man, and she doesn't understand how I need one special person. Sophie specifically says she would rather *I* was unhappy for the sake of *her* happiness.

It's difficult to know how to cope with Sophie's reaction to Gary. Friends try to advise but... One said: 'Get him in the house. She has to get used to him.' Another said: 'Keep him right away.' No one else in my circle is widowed. Some are divorced or have chosen to be alone, and they mainly have a low opinion of men. I don't, and I want to try again. Gary is not the one, though.

I've still got Frankie's ashes. Poor Gary doesn't know they are in the bedroom in a little chest. When I die, I would like to be cremated and have my ashes spread with Frankie's. I went to see a tarot-card reader, and he said: 'Your husband was your soulmate. He knows that whoever you are going to be with, he is only lending you. He wants you back.' I said: 'I want *him* back.' He is irreplaceable. I never thought I would find myself taking this road.

Life is for living. That is one lesson I have learnt. Sometimes I think my life is over. Other times, I feel it is an adventure. It is lovely being part of a couple and so secure, but it does become mundane. I do feel guilty saying this, but now I'm going out and meeting people, not always nice people, I'm seeing a slightly different side of things. It all adds to the richness of my life.

Ken's story

Ken was in a long-term gay relationship. His partner died of cancer. He has become involved with someone else.

Stuart and I were together twenty years. It was the only full-on relationship I ever had. He died of cancer at forty-one, just over eighteen months ago. It came out of the blue. We ran a company together and were in the middle of downsizing our lives by moving to the country. Suddenly he became ill. I thought he had fallen out of love with me because he felt bad about himself and he didn't know why. By the time he was diagnosed, the cancer had gone to his bowel. He died in the most beautiful way, at home, looking out of our window.

When Stuart died, every cell in my body was crying out for someone to fill every function he did. I found myself alone in a large four-bedroom house. My learning curve of running our company was vertical. Four months ago, I met Vix. He had just come out of a ten-year relationship. He still feels attached, and he can't commit to me at the moment. He doesn't know where he is at, jumping from one relationship to another. It was awful for me.

Last night, I lay in bed with Vix's legs wrapped around me, and it felt secure and nice. I know there is no such thing as security. I know that I have had that before and it has gone. Nothing is for ever. We have admitted that we won't be doing the partnership thing, certainly not in the near future. I know that Vix really does not tick the boxes for me. Why should he? Maybe it is for the best. I think if somebody had jumped into Stuart's shoes and I carried on where I had left off, there would have been some massive backlash.

My bereavement really only started properly when I met Vix. It threw up an amazing amount of emotions that I had not confronted before. Watching television while holding hands, stroking each other's necks – that sort of thing is going to set off a whole range of responses. I did not bargain for these feelings. It isn't a question of guilt. Even though it hurts, I have this amazing need to have somebody there to be intimate with. Before Stuart died, although he did try, he wasn't in a good enough state to be able to have that type of relationship. He was in a hospital bed and I was sleeping on the floor. It was difficult.

I have such fond memories of Stuart that I think I do make some comparisons between Vix and him. Vix is very different in lots and lots of
ways. There are some little responses that are the same, and I will be
thinking: 'Oh, very Stuart-like.' If I mentioned this to Vix, though, I
know he would be upset. I know Stuart would be very on for me to be
with somebody else, although we didn't talk about the possibility of
another partner when he was dying. We talked about the funeral and he
did say: 'I wonder what will happen to you when I have gone?' But I
could not imagine life without him.

When we first met, Stuart told me he could not be monogamous. I
found this difficult to take on board, but he explained 'how the freedom
you take is a freedom that you give'. We agreed on this. On holiday, if
something happened, it happened. We could talk about it, or not, and it
was fine. A lot of people cannot deal with this. At the end of the day, this
meant we could never be adulterous. In a funny way, it kept us more
together. For us, it was natural.

Vix feels threatened about my old relationship with Stuart. He does
not want me to think about him. Any talk of love makes him want to run a
mile because he does not know where he is at. He is totally free in other
ways. Anything goes. We ring each other every day and see each other a
couple of times a week. I think we are good catalysts for one another. I
think we do love one another in a way. I finished it twice, but there is this
amazing attraction between us.

It is not to do with Vix and having a new relationship. It is to do with
me. With anybody that came along, it would be the same. As soon as Vix
came along, I thought: 'This is great', and I nearly squeezed the life out of
the relationship by holding on so hard. I am incredibly needy.

Some people feel I should have waited a more reasonable amount of
time before starting with someone new. I did have a fling quite soon after
Stuart died. It only lasted a few weeks. Some people commented: 'He's
half your age; it's a bit soon', but my real friends just wanted to get me
sorted out. The fact is that Vix is not doing the job. He is quite
self-obsessed himself because of his own past. I find myself helping *him*.
He has never sat down and said to me: 'How do *you* feel now?' I lent him a
CD of Stuart's songs, but he could not play it. He doesn't want to know
about me and Stuart.

I am adopted and only have my elderly mother left now in my family.
Losing Stuart, I have lost everything. My relationship with him was
amazing. When we first got together, people told us we said we loved
each other too often. But we meant it. I would leave home to go to work,
and I would be halfway down the road and ring to say: 'Did I say that I
loved you?' After he died, although initially I did drink and overeat, I
thought I had dealt with things well. I thought I had done a good job of
my grief. I had a massive circle of friends, I went on holiday with new
friends, and I really reinvented myself. I am even about to climb the
shoulder of Everest. I thought I had but... Then Vix came along. It was
emotional and romantic and took me up in the air, only to find I was left
hanging there. I was sold on this man and had decided to blow the whole
lot on him. It does *not* feel nice to be with somebody who doesn't want to
live with you or be with you more. It is a hard lesson to learn. I thought I
had cracked it, but I had forgotten about the romance bit, the love bit.

Vix does not have as much money as me. He would be better off
moving into my flat, but he doesn't think it is the right thing to do. At
least he is totally honest. I do think we get what is right for us. I am quite
philosophical. Vix is very affectionate and very much there within given
parameters. But he is not my partner.

Stuart is still present in my life. I have had significant dreams which
have confirmed that sort of thing to me. A friend said to me: 'Stuart was
such a big character, such a massive part of your life, you are never going
to get somebody who is going to tick all that at once. At the moment, Vix
is ticking some, but not all. Maybe you need half a dozen people to get all
those functions sorted.' What I do get from Vix is affection, a great sex life
and adventure. Other friends are there for me in other ways that Vix is
not.

I am quite a spiritual person. I have studied Buddhism and Hinduism
and I teach yoga. I'm not certain about Heaven, but I don't think that life
finishes. I think it's a continuum. Stuart went because it was his time to go.
After spending so long together, fifty per cent of me is him. He is alive in
me. I am guided by most of his thoughts anyway. I can almost hear him
counselling me, saying: 'Don't do it that way, do it this.' I can hear him
saying: 'Don't get hung up about this guy.' But you wake up in the
morning and your hormones are raging...

I used to say, even when he was alive, that I did not think Stuart had a bad bone in his body. But I am quite pragmatic. I think goodness came naturally to him, but I don't think he was perfect. There were some things where I would think 'Bloody hell, Stuart…' Sometimes, in my head, I can hear Stuart telling me how to do things, but I think: 'I won't. I'll do them how I want.'

We were open about our relationship, but we did not go on about it. When he died, people would say: 'I am sorry to hear your friend has died.' I would say: 'He was not my friend. He was my partner.' They didn't see me as a widower. We may have been more constant and been together longer than a heterosexual couple, but it was not recognised. Because Stuart and I had space around us, people would not understand that either, and would devalue the relationship. I think it strengthened it. There wasn't a piece of paper and no children, but we were bound to each other. But I must say that when Stuart was dying, the hospital staff were very understanding. There was the recognition that I was the most important person to him.

I had never seen anybody die before. When he did die, we had Buddhist music playing, telling him to let go. I am not frightened of death after watching him. It made me more determined to get every bit of energy out of life. I had moments of deep depression, but I am somebody who says 'Get on with it.' I am quite hard on myself. I am only beginning to surface.

When Stuart died, people expected some big ritual about his ashes, but I just threw them into the wisteria, which is what he wanted. I did the Buddhist thing: he had died at 3.30 on Saturday, so the following week, I put a candle in front of his picture and meditated and cried. I did the same thing the following week until the seventh week. It takes that long before the soul is reborn. In the summer, we had a celebration of his life. People want you to mark further anniversaries, but I feel I have done it. Within a couple of weeks, I was down at the local shop, giving away his clothes. It didn't help that they put them on a mannequin in a window. We had a portrait done of us on our tenth anniversary. I have given this to a friend to put in her house because I felt anybody that came round, particularly Vix, would be trying to live up to Stuart's image. I got rid of the bed. I felt it had this 'couple thing' going on in it. It is time to leave this house now.

If anybody comes into the house, they would not know he exists. I am happy to talk about him. The more I talk, the better I feel. Things surface; I deal with them.

It is the same when Vix and I talk. We realise we mean quite a lot to each other. I don't think it is good to sit back, Miss Haversham-like, and to have all things from the past held sacred. To be honest, I do love change. This is not the change I wanted, but it has happened and I have to deal with it. I could walk out of the house with nothing and it would not bother me. I have the memories.

I went to have my tarot read, and he said: 'You have had a very positive, solid relationship and it has gone. He is telling you to move on. There will be a golden relationship around the corner.' It made me think: 'Yes, life does go on and it is pretty damn good, ultimately.' Every now and then, I think, you have to count your blessings. The times I think I am doing well are when I don't look at what I have lost but what I still have. Things are pretty bad, really, without Stuart, but there are some things that are better without him. The company has moved on because he is not there. Other people have come in. I am finding out all sorts of things about myself that he was protecting me from. You only learn through suffering. I have had a lot of suffering and I am learning a lot.

Tim's story

Tim is a widower who is now in a relationship with Sarah, his wife's best friend. He has two young girls and a boy and Sarah has two young boys.

My wife Anya and I came together in a summer romance. We didn't think it was going to last because we were from different cultures, but once we were married we tried hard to make it work. We were married for twelve years and had two girls, who were four and nine, and a boy, who was six. Then Anya was diagnosed with leukaemia. When she became ill, a lot of people helped care for her and us, but Sarah, Anya's best friend, was probably the most involved.

I couldn't come to terms with Anya's illness. I'm afraid, in the beginning, I avoided talking to the doctors and left Sarah very much in charge. I used the excuse of looking after the children to detach myself. They did need looking after, but I couldn't face the reality of losing Anya. I had lost my mother to cancer and hadn't really got over it. I don't think I ever really grieved my mother properly. Anya's illness was so sudden. Gradually, I began to realise that she might not live. Right up until the end, I hoped she was getting better and we clutched at every straw possible to keep her alive.

Anya and I talked about what would happen after she died. She said she wanted me to have a relationship again. I think it is quite common for people, women more than men, to try to find their own replacement. Anya's main reason for doing this was the children. She talked about a few of our women friends but specifically thought of Sarah, because she was the closest to us both. Knowing it was somebody she approved of made life easier when it did happen. Despite her advice, I didn't feel she was telling me what I had to do, and naturally I made my own choice.

As I was only in my early forties, the idea of moving on to another relationship felt natural. I don't know if I would have felt differently if Anya hadn't given me permission. When I knew she was going to die, I did start looking around me at other women, although I felt very guilty about this. At the hospital, they gave me this counsellor, who was only about twenty-two. I was looking at her and found myself wondering: 'Do I fancy you?' I would never have thought like this before Anya became ill. I might have thought: 'Oh, she's nice', but nothing more. Now I was looking at women, but it was not for her to be a mother to the children or anything like that. I wanted to find someone for me, for sex only. Anya and my lovemaking had dwindled because she was so ill and, although I desired her, it would have been dangerous. I still had sexual needs. I think I was also scared of being lonely.

Soon after Anya died, I registered on this website for bereaved people. It was just people chatting amongst themselves. This woman was saying how she'd met someone new but the person she really wanted was six feet under. I knew how she felt because, even if my marriage wasn't perfect, it was for life. I do not think I am glorifying what it was. The difficulty is that it didn't have an end. There is an end in a divorce and both people are still alive. You can have negative feelings towards that other person for what they have done to you. My marriage to Anya did not have an end.

Even though Anya had talked about Sarah and I coming together, it was a bit of a shock when it happened only a month after Anya died. I was prepared for her death in a way, but it was still a very strange time. When she was dying, and afterwards, there was all this love in the air – not just for Anya. I can't really explain it – Sarah and I felt this love for each other. Then, the guilt came in. Maybe this is why I tried to turn away from love and make our relationship purely physical. My undermining of our love at that stage confused us both. I started to question whether it was love or just physical. Were we just comforting each other? Sarah had not opened up to anybody since her children's father had left her, so this was also a significant moment for her too. I did, however, feel she loved me, and this made it feel all right. I do love her, but I have found it difficult to express this. I do not think I have got over Anya's death yet.

People warn you of the pitfalls of getting together so quickly. I haven't really felt there is a problem, although I know Sarah does. I think it's much more in the male psyche to move on. You don't see many widowers on their own for long. In fact, see a widower, see hundreds of women around. They're like bees to a honey pot. Soon after Anya died, a relative stranger actually asked me in the street whether I had found someone yet, as their daughter was interested. I think there are more difficulties for women in moving on. When I looked at the WAY Foundation list [see Useful contacts], I saw that it was eighty per cent women. I can't believe it is only men that have died.

The first step towards moving away from Anya and moving on was forcing myself not to sleep in our bedroom. Then I realised it was important to leave the house that we had lived in together. I had to let go of it. Getting to this point has taken me three years. Even now, there are still silly things I have not done, like changing my bank account. It has still got her name on it. I think: maybe when I have to move house, I'll change my address, my bank, everything else, and deal with it all in one go. I don't carry a photograph of Anya, but Sarah does. I never did. I don't have one of Sarah either. I carry a picture of the children, that's all. When we move to our new house, I think it will be the children who put up photographs of her. I don't know whether I should. I have a black-and-white one of our wedding day, which somebody gave us as a wedding present an hour after we got married. I don't know whether Sarah would find it hard to see that around all the time.

If Sarah hadn't known Anya, I think I would talk about her more. Apart from my counsellor, there are not many people I talk to about Anya. There are various friends who knew her, but I am worried about what Sarah would feel if I was with them all the time. If people ask about my past and Sarah is not around, I do mention Anya. I find that I do not say 'my late wife', I say 'my wife'; I forget to tell them she's dead. It seems irrelevant. I find I can't talk about my past, the things I've done, the places I've been, without including Anya, so I talk to people as if she's around.

I want to take the children to see their mother's family, but Sarah is concerned that it is divisive of the new family we are trying to create. I can understand how she feels, but I feel it is important to be supportive of Anya's family. Sarah says these things should evolve naturally and for all the children to get to know the 'new family'. She does not follow my argument that, in a divorce, it would be natural for the children to be taken to the separate families. I don't want to be confrontational, so I avoid it. Because of all the suffering I've known, I find avoiding things very easy.

More and more, however, as Sarah becomes increasingly part of my life, new memories are created and Anya goes out. You forget a little, although the old memories are always there. The new and the old are moving away from each other. It is not that I feel I have to cut with the past because of Sarah, but I have to do it for myself – and the children. Sarah does, however, find it difficult that I do hold onto the past. I think she feels that Anya's presence is still very much around, whereas she would not be if we were divorced. This question of possessions is confusing. Anya had some jewellery of my mother's that I had given to her. Sarah said she would like something of Anya's as her friend, but I feel, however, I should give all of it to the girls when they are older, as she was their mother.

Sarah often feels unhappy that I don't say any positive things to her, but I don't recall if I ever said them to Anya. It's difficult to say three years on, but maybe I did praise her more. I am not a very praising person. Before Anya died, I never praised the children as much as I do now. I've learned this from Sarah. In fact, I have learned from her more about how to be a parent. I think the children are having a more stable time, especially the little ones, than they ever had, because Anya was very up and down. I know I am changing being with Sarah. I do things the way she does when I am at her house. You adapt to anybody if you're living with them. You both adapt.

I do not think I compare the two of them. It's Sarah who does the comparing. Maybe that's because she knew Anya. I think she feels very insecure about the situation. This is why she needs reassurance about how there may be areas where she is better than Anya. She worries that I may be still thinking of Anya when we are in bed together. As they were friends, Anya told her things about us as a couple, and now Sarah can imagine the two of us together too graphically. But I never think of Anya sexually now. There are no images left. I really don't have an inner voice saying one is better than the other. I think of it as a totally different life now.

I still love Anya, but I don't think about Anya every day. I don't think I could ever replace that love I had for her. Neither do I feel I am being disloyal to her being with Sarah, because it is a different kind of love. It is not the same as my relationship with Anya, which was for life. Sarah is very independent and she doesn't want to marry. I'm not yet ready to marry Sarah, either. I sometimes wonder, if we did, if it would symbolise the end of my marriage to Anya. It's not that I still feel married to Anya, because then I'd be cheating on her. I don't feel married at all. What I do feel like is a single person – with children. Sarah sometimes says it would be better if I had had relationships with other people so that she didn't feel I was coming fresh from Anya to her. But, if I ever did this, I think she would be very upset.

Maybe neither of us has properly grieved Anya. The reason I first went to a counsellor was to deal with my grief, but we have not been talking about that for a long time now. It's more about my relationship with Sarah, the children, my parents, my father, my brother – all the other things going on in my life. My grief for Anya has moved more onto the back burner because life is going on and three years have passed.

Sarah made a promise to Anya that, somehow, she would take care of her children and, to a certain extent, both of us think of the relationship as being more for the children than for us. Having said that, I think our relationship is good most of the time. I think, though, that Sarah wants a bit more from the relationship than I can give yet. It's slowly coming out of me. Sometimes I feel I want to run away and live without anybody, to start all over again. But I can't with three children in tow. I think if we didn't have the children, we might have split up by now. You do kind of keep it together for them, and you make the best of it at the same time.

I think there are different types of love. There is the kind of love you have when you're young and there's really 'grown-up' love. As you get older and life makes more demands on you, love changes. Creating a new relationship while grieving and looking after children is a real balancing act. When Sarah and I were first together, neither of us was working and we created time for each other. Now that we have moved on and are immersed in daily life, we are not doing that. I am aware that we should again. But we have to accept these difficulties as part of being adult.

The children were very jealous initially. My eldest, Isabella, wanted me for herself. She was full of anger, anyway, angry at life. She made it very obvious she did not want me to be with Sarah. She felt I was betraying Anya. I told her that Anya had told me to move on and how she had thought Sarah was someone I could be with. Isabella has mellowed and recently has come round to thinking things aren't so bad. In fact, I think she is happier than she has ever been. Sarah has two boys, so we suddenly found ourselves with this huge family. At times, it feels as if Sarah is more bonded with *my* children than I am with *hers*. Although, the other day, when I was offered three cinema tickets for my children, I automatically said: 'We can't go, there's five of us.' That felt natural. My family has not been very supportive of Sarah and I. I don't know what I was expecting of them, but I feel they should be supportive of Sarah and what she has done for me and the children. Anya's family are more positive.

People haven't been openly critical about Sarah and I getting together, but we have felt self-conscious. Funnily enough, I haven't naturally socialised with my friends and Sarah. When my friends invited her to a party, I told them she was busy. In fact, she would have come, but I realised I hadn't wanted her to. This was because I wasn't ready for Sarah to be at a party where there would be lots of people who knew me with Anya. Despite what she said, I felt that Sarah wouldn't have found it easy either. I would let her come now. Time has elapsed.

I think about the next life and wonder where Anya is. I still feel I have unfinished business with Anya. We hadn't finished our life together. I can't imagine who I would want to be with when I die. At the moment, it's Anya, because Sarah's still alive. I know this is a cop-out. I know I have been confused and very difficult to live with. I feel I am healing now. One of the happiest moments I have had since Anya died was when we were all in the car going off somewhere together. I really liked that feeling. It felt symbolic of accepting being in my new life. People see us as one big family. That makes me happy. Bringing it all together feels like an achievement, which would not be possible without Sarah.

Sarah's story

After the death of her best friend, Sarah became the new partner of her friend's husband, Tim. She has two sons of her own, and Tim has two girls and a boy.

Anya and I had been best friends for twelve years. She had just married Tim when I met her. When she became ill, I was intimately involved with nursing and looking after her. During this time, Tim and I felt more and more close to each other. Six weeks after she died, we were together.

In the beginning, it felt beyond our control. I felt that Anya knew this would happen. Before she died, we had had a conversation where she told me who she would like Tim to be with, and she mentioned me. She even gave me warnings and advice about how to cope with Tim. She asked me to be a guardian to her children, although I knew I had to be there for her children anyway. Somehow, I also had a feeling Tim and I would be together. There was such a strong feeling in the air. I could see it in his eyes. It felt quite beautiful. There was a haze around. Her last words were, as she held both our hands, 'You must…Sarah', whatever that meant. It could have meant that we should be together or just that we should be there for each other as friends. Who knows?

I was the one who had to tell Tim that Anya was about to die. I remember him bringing the children into the hospital. Anya could just about open her eyes and she said to them: 'I can't believe how you become more and more beautiful each time I see you.' Her children had been somewhat abandoned during her illness, which compounded previous insecurities they had. They were extremely unruly and, although I had known them all those years, they were rather difficult to love, but I knew I had to look after them. It was shocking to see them watch their mother die. They just looked on in horror at the end of the bed.

As a mother, I had to allow a shift in the use of my time. My own children understood it was necessary, and I had to leave them at home with my mother. Friends told me I had to keep helping as there was no one else. Both Anya's and Tim's mothers had already died.

After Anya died, I had not really thought about *how* I would look after her children. I thought something would evolve. When Tim and my relationship changed into something else, it was quite a shock. It was so soon after her death. I remember how he kept asking me to come over before the funeral and wondering why. I did know he had an inner battle going on. At both the funeral and the memorial, I think he was confused about allowing me to sit near him. He wanted the comfort but placed this very large coat between us, creating some physical separation for the sake of respectability.

Then, one Friday, he was upset and crying. I remember touching his foot to pat it and he pulled me towards him. At the door, he held me and kissed me on the lips, not a proper kiss. I asked a friend after: 'Is it normal to kiss someone goodbye on the lips?' I was feeling confused. This was Anya's husband. How could this be?

That Christmas, I went to stay with him at his parents' house. Everything felt so different. I had been used to just dedicating myself to my children for seven years since their father had abandoned us. I was not used to socialising. That night, he was very physical. His attitude was: 'Why not?' I tried to slow things down. Looking back, I think it was all too soon. I am only now beginning to understand the link between grief and the need to be soothed through the physical senses. But it has to be said that I did want him too. We would often end up in tears and grieve in bed together. Anya was mentioned very often by both of us. Obviously, it brought intimate memories back for him, which he would recount and, as Anya and I had spoken so freely, I already knew these stories. Initially, this felt alright but it grew to haunt me. Obviously, when I was young, I had lots of boyfriends, as you do, and it wasn't confusing changing partners. This haunting used to become quite intrusive at times when Tim and I were in bed together. I would get the 'Anya thoughts'. It wasn't that I felt disloyal to her or guilty having her husband. I just felt second-place and felt that she had been more beautiful. Tim did not say anything to make me feel more beautiful or better.

It took a long time for this to change. Initially, it was soothing for both of us that she *was* there. I feel she would be happy for me to be with her husband. I can imagine her saying: 'Enjoy each other's bodies.' I know it was what she wanted, but it was *very* odd. I was uncomfortably aware that the last person he had touched was Anya, and I found this disturbing. I wished there had been another person in between. It felt as if he still belonged to her.

After that initial weekend, he wanted to do lots of things together, but then, suddenly, he turned off like a light. It was awful. He would come and see me, and then I would not hear from him for days. A while later, he would ring up and laugh it all off, and we would end up together again. After we had made love, he would say: 'I don't love you, I love Anya.' Or he would immediately talk about the children to cut out any romantic feeling. It was purely physical on his part. I know now this was through guilt. He needed to deny his feelings for me. He couldn't even open his eyes when he was making love to see who I was. That was when the fantasies set in that he was thinking of her in bed. I used to get very upset about it. I don't know why I stayed with him when I was being treated like this. Maybe it was because I could see he was not a truly horrible person, that he was wrecked by grief. Also, I had seen his huge capacity to care and be loving with Anya during her illness. Another factor was that I was beginning to see the potential of a big family as a happy thing. Really, I should not have put up with it at all. To make matters worse, Tim kept maintaining there was no future in our relationship. It was so destructive. I feel it would have been better for him to have been rampant as I hear some widowers are. He wasn't the type to sleep around, but he did need the physical side for comfort.

The good thing about our situation was that we were able to grieve for Anya together. I worried that he was blocking some of his grieving and I encouraged him to go to counselling. I found it easier to grieve when he was not around. I still can't believe she has died, my young friend dead, dreadful, shocking: the horror of her death and the pain. Then there is this other feeling, the excitement of a relationship, which moves her away a little bit.

After her death, I have got to know her in a different way, clearing up some of her unfinished business. Before, it wasn't necessary for me to become involved with differences in the way we mothered our children. I accepted her as my dearest friend. I know that *her* mother had committed suicide, and this had a knock-on effect on Anya's ability to mother. I feel bad criticising her. I also know I sometimes do it so that Tim will reassure me that I am better in some way. Tim does not really criticise her, as he feels very guilty doing so. I think it is very easy to glorify someone once they have died. Both of us did it in different ways. It took Tim a long time to acknowledge truthfully some of her human frailties, which we all have.

A major difficulty is that he is not able to make me feel superior to her in *any* way. I know he still loves her. I feel confused, as I remember how he used to ooze love towards her. In the last months, when I was sitting next to Anya's hospital bed, I saw them lying there together like two spoons. However, I would not respect him if he *didn't* still love her. People tell me he loves me dearly, but I don't actually see that. Sometimes, I feel as if I am filling a gap, I am functional. I knew that I fulfilled an important role looking after his children, talking about Anya and her family. Sometimes, I was acting as his counsellor. I wish he could have had more time between us and learnt to be alone, not had me as a distraction. I suppose this is very male.

He says that our relationship is important to him, but for a long time I felt that, because of his grief, he didn't have the mental space to really care for me. It was almost as if he could not receive anything from me, verbal or non-verbal; neither could he give out. He thought he was open but his shutters were down. Everything revolved around him for a very long time. I even felt I didn't have a right to be ill myself because it would remind him and the children of Anya. It has taken a long time for this to equalise and for there to be a more balanced situation. Now that the crisis has eased and things are up and running, is my job done?

Sometimes, I feel jealous of their past together. It is difficult knowing their inside story. Perhaps, if I hadn't known her, it would be easier. Their home used to be a sanctuary when I went there as her friend, but after she died, I found it hard going there. Seeing all the photographs of them together somehow negated what had developed between Tim and I. It made me see Tim belonging to Anya and her world. If he was a stranger, I would see them both as individuals. I would have known he had had a wife but I would not have known the essence of her. I would not have had a picture of her in my mind. I know precisely what Tim liked about Anya physically, and this kind of thing can 'haunt'. In my insecure moments, I amplify her positive aspects and forget her negative side. Strangely enough, Tim says he can't even remember their physical relationship now. I also went through phases of thinking that I loved Anya more than I loved Tim, and I was trying to attach to her through him. You name it, I have thought it.

The good thing about having known Anya is that I can understand more why her children react in certain ways. Sometimes, I think it would be easier if he had been divorced. Then he would be able to say to me: 'You are so much better than... It's a relief to be with you.' This would be reassuring as his divorced wife would be less of a threat.

It is very embarrassing when people make statements about it being too soon. It is already difficult enough, feeling you are in somebody else's place. At the funeral, however, Anya's sister asked if there was any chance that Tim and I would get together. This seemed shocking at that time and place. Although other people did pass judgement, I was most guilty of judging myself. When I went with him to visit his family for the first time, I felt as if it should be Anya sitting there, not me. Being in the front seat of his car with the children in the back, I felt that was *her* place. Tim did not seem to be uncomfortable about this. He didn't notice or didn't care. Maybe men close doors quicker. I think some of his friends found his ease shocking. Maybe Tim was displacing or soothing his grief, but this is quite hard for other people to understand. It doesn't feel good to be judged or out on view. I was used to seeing myself as a single parent, always alone. I knew my world had to change if I wanted this relationship, but change can bring its own grief. I know that we can't guarantee what is going to happen next. It didn't help, however, when a psychotherapist told me that she didn't hold much hope for our relationship because of its speed. Somehow, I feel that we might be different.

The most important thing is that we have allowed the children time to blend together. They have set the pace and we have followed on behind. We took things very slowly. We kept our relationship as private as we could for a long time and did not tell them initially. We never woke up in the same bedroom together. It felt right to protect them and to slowly allow the relationship to emerge. Those early days were more romantic, because if he visited, it was to see me. Now we are immersed in our big family and there is very little time for each other.

When his eldest daughter, Isabella, first realised about us, she was very upset. She put up all sorts of obstructions. She tried to drive me away. I remember how she tried to control her brother and sister, preventing them from coming too close to me. There were times when they wanted to visit me and she forbade them from doing so. She told them I would never be their mummy. I was discussing her being upset with my son, and he said: 'The problem is that Tim is still wearing his wedding ring.' I pointed out that he had never worn one. My son said: 'He is wearing one in his mind.' Several months later, when she had warmed to me, I asked my son if Tim was still wearing his wedding ring. He said: 'No, he has taken it off.'

The children do not seem to find the situation confusing now. They are very happy together as a group. They seem to think that as Anya is dead, Tim can love someone else and are very natural about it. This summer, Isabella was asked by a little boy what happened to her mum. She explained that her mum had died but then said: 'Sarah's my mum now.' I found this very moving. When Tim's youngest had to write about herself for a school project, she wrote: 'I live with my mum and dad and my big family. My mum died and we got involved with Sarah's family. I have three brothers and one sister.' This has been completely spontaneous from her, as we are not married. For children, bereavement is devastating and painful, but it is not the same type of hurt as divorce.

We used to talk to the children about Anya a great deal, because I felt it was important to keep her with us. As our everyday lives have moved on, however, we seem to talk about her less, as they are grieving less. We still have ceremonies where we remember her, like letting off balloons on her birthday, and we have her photograph in the living room. It is important that Tim's children have connections with their past, but I did feel uneasy when Tim wanted to take his children to Anya's family without us. It has been hard enough trying to create a unified family and I felt it would have been better if we all went together.

My own children and I have had to go through a period of adapting. My son always said his worst fear was for us all to get together. Isabella replied her worst fear was that her mum would die. We now talk very openly about death, but they are always going to have different perspectives. If I am really honest, I cannot yet feel the unconditional love for his children that I feel for mine. There is no reason to feel this love instantly. It is something which grows. I feel that my children were incredibly generous in sharing me. They felt sorry for Tim's children. Initially, because of his grief, Tim didn't have room in his mind for my children, but, as this has subsided, they have grown fond of him. We feel like one big family with a few cracks.

At the end of the day, I can see all three of us laughing together in Heaven, wherever that is. Bringing our two families together has sometimes felt like stepping into a broken picture and learning how to tread on the shards. Despite everything that's gone on between Tim and I, there is harmony now. I can almost imagine us pottering about together in our old age. This must be strange for him, as he had imagined being with Anya in his old age. What we have been through, and the enormity of it, creates a very firm foundation for us to build on. I have seen his wisdom and his intuition.

Suzie's story

When she was in her twenties, Suzie married a widower, with older children, very soon after his wife died. Unfortunately, this relationship failed.

My relationship with a widower started within weeks of the death of his wife. It was a very heady time, and he seemed to have a great need for me. I immediately fell pregnant. This was a real dilemma as we were in such a taboo situation. Although I wanted to have the baby, he felt it was better to terminate it because he feared the reaction of his children and others.

We had a lot of difficulties after this, but we resolved them. We got married and I moved into their house. Our beautiful baby was born with learning difficulties. I really hoped all would go well with our new family. Unfortunately, I think our biggest mistake was that we did not move house. Another problem was that his older children were very angry and unfriendly towards me.

We are now divorcing after ten years. One of the major factors has been that he couldn't let go of his dead wife. Her study remains untouched to this day. Her books and photographs are still in exactly the same places as they were when she lived there. People tell me that there is a remarkable resemblance between his dead wife and myself, not only in looks, which even *I* can see, but in interests and artistic talent. I am an artist myself, and so was she. This makes me feel as though he has just looked to replace her with a replica. This is a very hard feeling to live with. I can no longer live in her shadow.

Esther's story

Esther was divorced and then married a widower, who died recently. She is in her late sixties.

There are different problems at different ages with bereavement and moving on. If someone is energetic and full of life, it is not the same as if they are really old. An older person might feel they have had their life. It might be a lonely life, but they have had a life. At sixty-eight, I'm somewhere in between. When Larry died, I did not have the energy to think positively about the future and rush around as we used to.

It was a shock. He had had cancer of the bowel but was in remission. Then he started to feel unwell. Following an MRI [scan], the neurologist informed us that he had secondaries and only had a matter of weeks. Larry had always been such a positive man, energetic and healthy, in fact, the healthiest of our very large circle of friends.

I met Larry and his wife when I was in a very unhappy marriage, very much on its last legs. When you are in this fragile state, if there's someone around who is '*simpatico*', the heightened emotion can bring people together. His first wife had been ill for several years and had become disabled. She was my dearest friend. She did not tell him how ill she was, because she did not want to worry him. She did not think he could face her illness very well. My first thought was: 'How would he manage without her?' As her friend, I was helping her and became closer to him. We became intimate soon after she died. It would be difficult to say when we realised there was a feeling between us. Maybe we denied this to ourselves for some time. We did not think of saying or doing anything while his first wife was alive.

People were very judgemental. It was upsetting and annoying. There was one old friend of theirs who, instead of being judgemental of *him*, which would have been more appropriate, rejected *me* and would not talk to me. It was not me that was having a relationship so soon after losing a spouse: it was him. But she would not have anything to do with me. Men seem to move on more quickly, and it is more accepted. Statistics show that happily married men are liable to move on and replace.

In previous times, when life was short and people often died at an early age, it was much more accepted that people married again. A man would need a woman to look after his children, a woman would need a man to support her, and so on. Life was very tough and people were more pragmatic, but now there is embarrassment. There is not the obvious necessity.

Remarriage can be a lifeline, but even then people can still be resistant. For example, I had a friend who had MS [multiple sclerosis]. His wife was very ill with cancer. When his wife died, he ended up forming a relationship with her nurse. Their daughter would have nothing to do with this new relationship and was, in fact, obstructive. You would have thought the family would have been delighted to have someone to look after him. He was fifteen years older than his new love. They ended up being married only a year before he died.

Although Larry and I were very in love, my parents would not have anything to do with him. They should have been fully aware that my marriage had broken down long before Larry was on the scene. It just 'happened' between us. Crisis does not give you warning. Some friends were judgemental, and this created a division between us. I think people should be allowed to make their own salvation.

I felt I had rather a lot to live up to. She was my good friend, a wonderful woman, a wonderful cook – it made me feel inadequate. It did not take me too long to get over that, because he told me that I was the love of his life. My first very strong feeling was that she would be so relieved that I was looking after him. She would be so pleased to know it was me and that there was somebody there.

Due to a series of accidents, we were thrown into living together more quickly than we anticipated. My marriage finally broke up and I was going to live in a room. Larry said: 'Everyone knows we are together, we are happy, what is the point of going to this grotty room?' I wanted to show that I did not leave my husband for his sake and that I could stand on my own two feet. Larry gave me the confidence to move into their house, but I felt very uncomfortable there. To make matters worse, my ex-husband went around saying I had left him for Larry.

It was difficult moving into their house because I felt her presence there. The house used to be my refuge before because she had been my shoulder to cry on. Now, I felt very uncomfortable there and felt it was her house, not mine. It had been full of her photos of them together. Eventually, we moved and this changed, but I think he always kept her photo in his wallet. It felt strange, because the house represented his two lives. I was only part of one of those lives.

I can understand why some people would think that getting together too quickly is a danger. I think it is a possibility for some people that they are running away from their grief. It seems that men seem to find it easier to cut from one relationship to another. It can be confusing. I have had bereavement counselling for a year and a half now. The counsellor was emphatic that there are *no* rules regarding the grieving process.

I watched this programme about Esther Rantzen trying to find another man after losing her husband. I was surprised that she could be so public about this. I was particularly shocked when the producers told her that if she wanted to find a new man, she should not wear her wedding ring. I found this disgusting, because it is negating their marriage. When you are divorced, you *want* to negate the marriage, but when you have a loving marriage, it is a badge of honour.

In a bereavement group I went to, I noticed that there were many women who formed relationships with the most ghastly of men. I can see that loneliness can lead to desperation and to very bad choices. It affects your sense of judgement. I've told myself I must never get into a situation where I would accept something I would not have accepted before, just because I am lonely. Although, when you have become used to being part of a very strong pair, it feels much more difficult to be without somebody. It is a very difficult balance – not to feel guilty contemplating having somebody else. I think 'Good luck to people who move on', but I'm very wary because I know the mistakes people make through desperation. It is more likely to happen to women rather than to men. Men will find women more naturally. Certainly in the older age group there are many, many more widows than widowers, and any man that is halfway decent will be snapped up quickly.

Another thing is that the men can go younger. I mean, younger women are still attracted to older men, but not vice versa. Because older women very often have been dependent on their men financially, they have few resources. They have not developed their own interests and have had their social life through their husband. When he dies, they are lacking in resources. In another way, though, men are more lost, because they have often become dependent on women to organise them and tend to have fewer friends. This may cause them to appear like a 'little boy lost' and this, in turn, can be very attractive to women. Women are often excluded socially because so many people play the numbers game. For example, at dinner parties, people are prepared to make an extra place for a man, whereas a spare woman will be regarded as a threat or a nuisance. A man alone will never have difficulty getting invitations.

I think there is nothing in the world worse than losing your soulmate. I think it is worse than divorce. I think it would be very difficult to separate if you felt you were soulmates. In my experience of divorce, it was a relief to be away from him. With bereavement, however, there is not that sense of failure you feel in a failed marriage. You are parted in death but not in love. You still have that love. Nothing can take it away.

I've been through all sorts of things, but nothing compares with the agony of bereavement. It leaves you physically and emotionally in shreds. At least we worked as a team before he died, so it was not a shock having to look after myself. It took me a long time to face it all though. Having to do the first tax return after he died was so painful. It brought home the fact that he was no longer here.

Just two weeks after Larry died, an extremely insensitive woman said: 'Oh, you won't be on your own for very long.' My grief was so raw – this seemed so wrong. I have a good male friend who makes me laugh. My mother was very impressed how caring he was. When she found out he was fifteen years younger, her reaction was: 'What a pity. You might have been able to get together.' What sort of remark was that, when I was in constant tears? Maybe people are comforting themselves somehow.

It all depends who they are and how they say it. A really good friend said: 'Maybe, one of these days, you'll be in Waitrose and you'll ask someone to get something off the shelf… Who knows? Maybe something just might happen.' I've got to the point, where, if it does, I'm prepared to accept it. I'm not looking.

But, whoever comes along next has got a lot to live up to, because Larry was larger than life. I loved the fact that he was very popular. People were round him like bees round a honey pot. I didn't mind because he always came home to me. After someone like him, anyone else is going to be boring.

Bernadette's story

Bernadette was widowed in her late forties when her husband was killed in a road-traffic accident. They had two teenage children. She is currently with a widower, who also has two children.

My husband, Desmond, died instantly at the roadside. He was knocked from his bike at traffic lights and fell under a lorry, which dragged him along. I was at work forty miles away on the day, and the police could not contact me to tell me what had happened. As time went on, I went to search for him at his work. As soon as I saw the police officer there, I sensed it was dreadful news.

My last few words to Desmond that morning had been something like 'I'm off.' I don't know if I even said goodbye. Luckily, because of our wonderful relationship, I knew how much we loved each other. I had to say goodbye at the chapel of rest before the funeral. What a cold way to part from someone I had known and loved for nearly thirty years and had two children with. All our years together, we never had an argument. The children were twenty and sixteen when he died.

My family, who were mostly in Ireland, came to the funeral in Manchester, and afterwards they could not do enough for us as a family. Since Desmond was from Zimbabwe, he had no family in this country, but two cousins were able to attend the funeral.

Two years after Desmond's death, I felt I was gaining strength and I felt the need to socialise again. I was even able to consider at least having a friendship with a man. I met Nick through a networking group and we just seemed to hit it off from our first meeting. We just felt good together. As he had lost his wife very suddenly four years earlier, we just seemed to have a bond almost right away. It was wonderful to be able to have an adult conversation again. This was something I missed so much after my husband's death.

I did find it difficult being close physically at first. Nick was most considerate and sensitive. We adapted, but it took me longer than him to adjust to us being close. I have only had this one relationship since my husband died, but I do think men and women grieve differently. Men seem to be able to leave the past behind more readily and do not seem to verbalise how they feel in the same way as women. But, no matter what, both men and women are influenced by the nature of their previous relationship.

I still talk about Desmond, my husband. His pictures are displayed in the living room. I talk privately to him before I go to sleep. I tell him what I have been doing that day and that I still love him. I also tell him about my relationship with Nick and how he is looking after me now. I feel very comfortable doing things in this way. It seems natural now for me to do this.

I never make comparisons. I decided this early on. Right at the beginning, I told Nick that he was not a substitute for my husband; nor was I a substitute for his wife. I also said my love for him was different from my love for my husband. Although he has not verbalised this, I know Nick's views are similar. I didn't say much about our relationship to other people for a while but, when I did, overall, they were very supportive to me. Nick has now met a number of my family and has recently travelled to Ireland to meet my mother. She is very happy for us both.

My two children are now in their twenties. My daughter and I talk about Desmond often, but my son does not find talking easy. In fact, he doesn't ever chat openly about his father. They have both left home now and don't say a lot about my new relationship with Nick. When I first told them, they said that I must do what I thought was right for me.

Nick has got two children of his own, who are now eighteen and fourteen. They seem to accept me but probably still see me as a visitor when I go to their house. I do keep my distance and do not get involved in discussions about the children. I show an interest in them but do not get involved in the day-to-day issues.

While I miss my husband greatly, I have managed somehow to adapt to life without him. I feel very fortunate to have met Nick. I have no idea what the long-term outcome of our relationship will be. For now, we just enjoy each other's company tremendously and are happy to see how things develop. We do not plan too much into the future. I'm sure, after loss, one is cautious, or even a little fearful, of being hurt again by further loss.

Nick and I have a very good understanding of each other's feelings about the past, both our partners having died in very sudden situations. He understands about loss as he has had a great loss in his life as well. We do not talk about death all that much, but just refer to our loved one when it seems appropriate.

My husband is buried in a plot for two people, and if I remain in the area I will probably be buried there with him. I have a strong religious faith so I believe I will meet my husband again in Heaven. I look forward to that very much, although I don't know what to expect by way of being able to recognise him. Not sure how he will look then!

Nick and I still live in our own houses, and this type of relationship seems to suit the both of us for now. Things may change in the future when the children are older. We are just living for now. There are no threats from the past whatsoever for either Nick or myself, and neither of us glorify our loved ones who have gone. We just chat about them, almost as if they were just away for a while and have been delayed in returning.

Epilogue

To be loved means to be consumed. To love is to give light with inexhaustible oil. To be loved is to pass away. To love is to endure.

(Rilke [1910] 1992)

Writing these chapters and interviewing these exceptional people has been a sacred lesson. It has been a lesson not about death but, rather, about human courage and resilience. Resilience and resourcefulness have carried these people through the stormy seas of grief. They have sunk to the depths of desperation, gradually wading through agony, until most have reached a point of relative calm. Above all, it has been a lesson about love.

Loss causes many reactions and responses, but there are no rules to abide by, just one common factor: grief. There is a strong sense of emptiness. In fact, the word 'widow' comes from the Sanskrit meaning 'empty'. Perhaps it is this emptiness that drives people to the next stage. How this grief is wrestled with is dependent on the individual and all that has gone before in that individual's life.

No matter how complete some may feel now, all those people interviewed still have immense affection for their first love. They feel connected to them. The second love could never be a substitute. Each love stands alone, loved and honoured in their own right. When the pain of loss subsides, hope and the good memories of love carry us to the next stage.

> We find a place for what we lose. Although we know that after such a loss, the acute stage of mourning will subside, we also know that we shall remain inconsolable and will never find a substitute. No matter what may fill the gap, even if it be filled completely, it nevertheless remains something else.
>
> *(Sigmund Freud, cited in Monaghan 1998)*

Love is deeper than life itself. It is beyond us and keeps us connected to the past, the present and the future. In spite of all of today's concern with the material side of life, love keeps affirming itself as the existence of the soul. Through the ages, all cultures have honoured the immense spiritual value of love. Love is the core of life and death and is also the force that creates new life after loss. In this book, each person's journey through this experience of love and loss has been unique and intensely personal.

Judgement from those around can pierce with poisonous arrows of doubt. Surviving this ordeal requires people to reach into their souls and search for strength.

> There is nothing in this world either good nor bad but thinking makes it so.
>
> *(Hamlet, Act II, Scene II)*

Before you can overcome suffering, there will be dilemmas, there will be pain, there will be stops and starts. There is joy waiting for you, but it is being masked by the suffering. Not everyone will find it easy to remove this mask. Every human being has a desire for happiness and a wish to overcome suffering. This is quite justified. We have a natural right to achieve as much happiness as possible, and we also have the right to overcome suffering.

> Only those who avoid love can avoid grief. The point is to learn from it and remain vulnerable to love.
>
> *(John Branther, cited in Monaghan 1998)*

It seems that widows and widowers do remain vulnerable to love, perhaps because they are not so scarred by the negativity of a marital breakup. Perhaps their love may be arrested temporarily before it resumes to flow in two directions, the old love and the new.

Love itself is the essence of life. It stems from a well that does not run dry and is burrowed deeper by sorrow. When love starts to flow again in a new relationship, it can burst forth with renewed vigour from these new depths. This heals the scars of grief. This new depth of feeling will give another sense to it, being 'better to have loved and lost than never have loved at all'.

Starting to love a grieving person is like entering a broken picture. It is a unique situation to enter. The person you love still loves another. In no other situation would anyone be expected to accept this. This seems impossible, almost unreasonable, until the situation is understood in its entirety. Compassion from both sides is needed. Eternal love, even with all its beauty, can be threatening. To undo this threat will require under-standing that love has no limits. Many can be loved. All is possible with love.

References and bibliography

Abraham, K. (1924) *A short study of the development of the libido, viewed in the light of mental disorders.* In D. Biran and A. Strachey (eds) *Selected Papers in Psychoanalysis.* London: Hogarth Press, pp.418–452.

Benson, J. and Falk, A. (eds) (1996) *The Long Pale Corridor: Contemporary Poems of Bereavement.* Newcastle upon Tyne: Bloodaxe.

Bernard, J. (1969) 'Remarriage of the widowed and the divorced.' In R.S. Cavan (ed) *Marriage and Family in the Modern World,* 3rd edn. New York: Thomas Y. Crowell, pp.463–471.

Bowlby, J.A. (1988) *A Secure Base. Clinical Applications of Attachment Theory.* London: Brunner–Routledge.

Burks, V.K., Lund, D.A., Gregg, C.H. and Bluhm, H.P. (1998) 'Bereavement and marriage for older adults.' *Death Studies, 12,* 1, pp.50–60.

Du Maurier, D. (1938) *Rebecca.* London: Arrow.

Dunn, M. (2000) *The Good Grief Guide.* Oxford: Pathways.

Emerson, S. (ed) (2004) *In Loving Memory: A Collection for Memorial Services, Funerals and Just Getting By.* London: Little Brown.

Freud, S. (1949) *Mourning and Melancholia.* London: Hogarth Press.

Gallagher-Thompson, D., Futterman, A., Farberow, N., Thompson, L.W. and Timson, J. (1993) 'The impact of spousal bereavement on older widows and widowers.' In M.S. Strobe and R.O. Hansson (eds) *Handbook of Bereavement.* New York: Cambridge University Press, pp.227–239.

Gibran, K. (1997) *The Prophet.* Hertfordshire: Wordsworth Editions.

Glick, I., Weiss, R. and Parkes, C.M. (1974) *The First Year of Bereavement.* New York: John Wiley & Sons.

Goldberg, H. (1976) *The Hazard of Being Male.* New York: Signet.

Halpin, B. (2002) *It Takes a Worried Man.* London: Hamish Hamilton.

Jennings, E. (2002) 'Into the Hour.' In *New Collected Poems.* Manchester: Carcanet Press.

Kübler-Ross, E. (1977) *The Wheel of Life.* London: Bantam Books.

Kübler-Ross, E. (1997) *On Death and Dying.* Harlow: Prentice Hall & IBD.

Lewis, C.S. (1961) *A Grief Observed.* London: Faber and Faber.

Lieberman, M. (1996) *Doors Close, Doors Open.* New York: Putman.

Mantala-Bozos, K.I. (2003) 'The role of religion and culture on bereavement: the example of the Orthodox Christian tradition.' *Journal of Critical Psychology, Counselling and Psychotherapy, 3*, 2.

Monaghan, L. (1998) *Time to Say Goodbye.* Cambridge: Lutterworth Press.

Moss, M.S. and Moss, S.Z. (1980) 'The image of the deceased spouse in remarriage of elderly widow(ers).' *Journal of Gerontological Social Work, 3*, 59–70.

Moss, M.S. and Moss, S.Z. (1984) 'Remarriage of widowed persons: a triadic relationship.' In D. Klass, P.R. Silverman and S.L. Nickman (eds) *Continuing Bonds: New Understanding of Grief.* Philadelphia: Taylor & Francis, pp.163–176.

Neruda, P. (1994) 'Dead Woman.' In *The Captain's Verses.* (Translated by Brian Cole.) London: Anvil Press Poetry.

Picardie, J. (2001) *If the Spirit Moves You.* Basingstoke: Macmillan.

Rilke, R.M. (1992) [1910] *The Notebooks of Malte Laurids Brigge.* (Translated by M.D. Herter Norton.) New York: Norton. (Original work published 1910.)

Russac, R.J., Steighner, N.S. and Canto, A.I. (2002) 'Grief Work versus Continuing Bonds: A Call for Paradigm Integration or Replacement?' *Death Studies, 26*, 6, pp.463–478.

Schumacher, E.F. (1973) *Small is Beautiful.* New York: Harper and Row.

Silverman, P.R. and Klass, D. (1996) 'Introduction: what is the problem?' In D. Klass, P.R. Silverman and S.L. Nickman (eds) *Continuing Bonds: New Understandings of Grief.* Philadelphia: Taylor & Francis, pp.3–27.

Smith, S.C. (1999) *The Forgotten Mourners.* London: Jessica Kingsley Publishers.

Staudacher, C. (1991) *Men and Grief.* Oakland, CA: New Harbinger Publications Inc.

Stroebe, M.S. and Schut, H.A.W (1994) 'The dual process model of coping with bereavement.' Presented at The Fourth International Conference on Grief and Bereavement in Contemporary Society, Stockholm, Sweden, 12–16 June 1994.

Warwick, A. (ed) (2003) *The Nation's Favourite Poems of Remembrance.* London: BBC Books.

Zisook, S. and DeVaul, S.Z. (1976) 'Grief related facsimile illness.' *International Journal of Psychiatric Medicine, 7*, 329–336.

Useful contacts

The Compassionate Friends
53 North Street
Bristol BS 1EN
Helpline: 08451 232304
www.tcf.org.uk

A nationwide organisation for bereaved parents, offering understanding, support and encouragement after the death of a child.

Cruse Bereavement Care
Cruse House
126 Sheen Road
Richmond
Surrey TW9 1UR
Helpline: 0870 167 1677
www.crusebereavementcare.org.uk

Offers free bereavement support, advice and information to anyone bereaved by death.

Halley Stewart Library
St Christopher's Hospice
51–59 Lawrie Park Road
London SE26 6DZ
Tel: 020 8768 4500

2Higher Ground
PO Box 28
Tewkesbury GL20 6YZ
Tel: 01684 850456

Offers help to carers of cancer patients.

Lesbian and Gay Bereavement Project
Healthy Gay Living Counselling
24 Southwark Street
London SE1 1TY
Helpline: 020 7403 5969 (Monday, Tuesday, Thursday)

Trained volunteers offer a listening ear to lesbians and gay men who have been bereaved, as well as to family, friends and colleagues.

Merrywidow
www.merrywidow.me.uk

Website dedicated to advising young widows.

The National Association of Widows
3rd Floor
48 Queens Road
Coventry CV1 3EH
Tel: 024 7663 4848
www.widows.uk.net

The Natural Death Centre
6 Blackstock Mews
Blackstock Road
London N4 2BT
Tel: 0871 288 2098
www.naturaldeath.org.uk
Email: ndc@alberyfoundation.org

Advice and information on dying, funerals and bereavement.

Survivors of Bereavement by Suicide (SOBS)
Volserve House
14–18 West Bar Green
Sheffield S1 2DA
Tel: 0114 272 5955
www.uk-sobs.org.uk

The War Widows' Association of Great Britain
48 Pall Mall
London SW1Y 5JY
Tel: 0870 241 1305
www.warwidowsassocation.org.uk

WAY Foundation
PO Box 6767
Brackley
Northamptonshire NN13 6YW
Tel: 0870 011 3450
www.wayfoundation.org.uk
Email: info@wayfoundation.org.uk

Offers a self-help social and support network for men and women widowed
before the age of fifty, and their children.

Winston's Wish
Clara Burgess Centre
Bayshill Road
Cheltenham
Gloucestershire GL50 3AW
Helpline: 0845 20 30 405
www.winstonswish.org.uk

Supports children and young people following the death of their mum, dad,
brother or sister through a range of services, including an interactive website.

Subject index

acceptance
  of death 17
  of previous relationship 36–7
ageing, and sexual relationships 44–5,
  87
anger
  imagined 38
  of surviving partner 16–17, 21–2,
    49
animals' grief 16
Anne's story 82–5

The Bed 53–4
beliefs, 'Heaven' and afterlife 39, 82, 87,
  92, 94, 109, 132, 139
Belinda's story 105–7
Bernadette's story 137–9
Buddhism, mourning rituals 20, 119

carers and nurses, feelings towards 48,
  56, 99, 134
'caring' feelings
  and new relationship 26
  towards deceased partners 24–5,
    124, 126
  see also relationship with deceased
    partners
Catholicism, mourning rituals 18–19
changes
  impact on children 62–4, 131
  home environments 34–5, 69, 79,
    107, 108, 122
children 55–66
  confusion of grief 56–7
  coping with change 62–4, 131–2

feelings of resentment 57–8, 113,
  125, 130–1
finding 'replacement mothers' 121
and grandparents 27–8, 79, 123
grieving rituals 18, 28, 80, 131–2
identity and deceased parents 98
new families 27–8, 61–2, 76, 80,
  131–2
and parent's new relationships
  57–66, 90, 113, 125, 130–1
sole parenting responsibilities
  46–7, 50–1, 74–5, 110–1
Christianity, mourning rituals 18–19
Claire's story 76–80
commitment and loyalty
  and new relationships 28
  towards deceased partner 24–5,
    97, 124, 126
Compassionate Friends organisation 147
counselling 94
  for bereaved children 56–7, 63
cremation 93, 115
criticisms 67–72
Cruse Bereavement Care 147
crying 15

Dead Women (Neruda) 22
death, and learning 115, 132, 142–3
Death is Nothing At All (Scott Holland)
  29–30
deceased partners
  'blessing' new relationships 38–9,
    89, 128
  as former friends 36, 126–32
  and 'glorification' 35–6, 114–15,
    129
  parents and relations 27, 79, 90–1,
    107, 115, 123

deceased partners *cont.*
    personal belongings 34, 77,
      113–14
    photographs 27, 34, 77, 81, 87,
      106, 122, 130
    visualisations 29, 54, 76, 80–1,
      127–8
    see also relationship with deceased
      partners
defence mechanisms, and sex 49
depression 17, 105
displacement activities 48
divorce, versus bereavement 33, 80, 121,
  136
dying, stages (Kübler-Ross) 16–17

Elizabeth's story 98–9
embarrassed feelings 43
Esther's story 133–7

families
    being accepted 37–8, 78–9, 90–1
    deceased partners 24–5, 79, 90–1,
      123
    grandparents 27–8, 79, 123
    rates of grieving 35, 69
    restructuring 27–8, 61–2, 76,
      131–2
family occasions
    Christmas 127
    memories 26, 27–8, 81, 127–8
Fatma's story 109–11
fear of impotency 47
feeling inadequate 35–6
financial issues 83, 136
Freud, Sigmund 16, 142
friends
    expectations 79, 82
    reintroducing 125
    see also judgements and opinions

gay relationships 116–20
    and grieving 45, 48, 116–17
gender differences
    attitudes towards widowhood
      70–1, 91, 122, 136
    grieving 45–50, 50–2, 80,
      99,100–1, 135
    life expectancy following
      bereavement 50
    sexual drive 47
glorification 35–6, 114–15, 129
The Good Grief Guide (Dunn) 19
grandparents 27–8, 79, 123
Greek Orthodoxy, mourning rituals 19
grief
    culture and religious rituals 17–21
    gender differences 45–50, 50–2,
      80, 99, 100–1, 135
    'interrupted' 132–3
    physical symptoms 15
    stages (Kübler-Ross) 16–17,
      68–70
    and suicide 46
    timescales and rates 45–6, 69,
      76–7, 97, 135
'grown-up' love 125, 132
guilt
    and new relationships 45, 115
    of surviving partner 21–2, 45, 115
Gwyneth's story 102–4

Halitzah 20, 86
Halley Stewart Library 147
Hamlet (Shakespeare) 55–6, 142
The Hazard of Being Male (Goldberg) 48
health status following bereavement 49
'Heaven' 39, 82, 87, 92, 94, 109, 132,
  139
2Higher Ground 83, 147
Hinduism, mourning rituals 21

homes
    dead person's presence 34, 77
    making changes 34–5, 69, 79,
        107, 108
    and moving house 122–3

impotency fears 47
individual stories
    Anne's story 82–5
    Belinda's story 105–7
    Bernadette's story 137–9
    Claire's story 76–80
    Elizabeth's story 98–9
    Esther's story 133–7
    Fatma's story 109–11
    Gwyneth's story 102–4
    Kerri's story 88–92
    Lucia's story 112–15
    Mahmud's story 92–8
    Marilyn's story 73–5
    Richard's story 85–8, 100–2
    Simon's story 80–2
    Suzie's story 132–3
    Tony's story 107–9
information sources, bereavement and
    moving on 147–9
intimacy 24–5
    and new relationship 26–7
intimate moments
    deceased person's presence 38–9,
        76, 124, 127–8
    and 'not belonging' 76
    see also sexual relationships
Into the Hour (Jennings) 72
Irish Catholics, mourning rituals 18–19
Islam
    and the afterlife 39
    mourning rituals 20, 109–10
It Takes A Worried Man (Halpin) 47–8

jealousy 56, 103, 129–30
Judaism, mourning rituals 19–20, 85, 86
judgements and opinions 67–72, 95–6,
    130, 134, 142
    about bereaved women 70–1, 91,
        134–5

Kerri's story 88–92

learning through death 115, 132, 142–3
Lesbian and Gay Bereavement Project
    148
life coaching 83
life expectancy, following bereavement
    50
loss 141–2
    different coping strategies 68–9
    factors involved 68
    of 'soulmates' 112–15, 116–20
    see also grief
love after loss, epilogue 141–3
Lucia's story 112–15

Mahmud's story 92–8
making changes
    moving house 122–3
    to home environment 34–5, 69,
        79, 107, 108
Marilyn's story 73–5
marital bed, significance 49, 53–4, 79
mementoes and photographs 27, 35, 77,
    81, 84, 87, 106, 122, 130
memories
    and comparisons 37–8, 84, 90,
        95, 106, 117, 124, 138
    creating new ones 123
    and family occasions 26,27–8, 81,
        127–8
    'forever young' 76
    'good and bad' 74, 81, 84, 119

men and bereavement
    attractiveness to women 48, 51,
        78, 91, 136
    grieving 45–50, 97, 99, 135
    life expectancy 50
    sympathy towards 48, 51, 78, 91,
        136
    remarriage rates 75, 96, 122
Men and Grief (Staudacher) 46, 68
'merry widow' image 51–2
Merrywidow website 148
Merton, Paul 69–70
Mnemossina 19
money management 83, 136
Mormons 31
motherhood 50–1, 74
    finding 'replacement fathers' 98,
        103, 111
    finding 'replacement mothers' 121
mourning
    customs and rituals 17–21, 28, 74,
        80, 85, 86, 109–10, 119,
        131–2
    and tears 15
    timescales and rates 45–6, 69,
        76–7, 97, 135
    see also grief
moving house 122–3

The Natural Association of Widows 148
The Natural Death Centre 148
'new' families 27–8, 61–2, 76, 131–2
new partners
    feeling threatened 33–5, 84, 103,
        117
    initial feelings towards 21–2,
        26–9
    see also relationship with new
        partners
nurses and carers 48, 56, 99, 134

On Death and Dying (Kübler-Ross 1997)
    16–17
organisations 147–9

Papua New Guinea, mourning rituals 18
parenting responsibilities 46–7, 50–1,
    74–5, 110–1
photographs of deceased partners 27,
    35, 77, 81, 84, 87, 106, 122, 130
Platell, Amanda 69–70
Protestant faith 18–21

Quilliam, Susan 70

Rantzen, Esther 135
Rebecca (Du Maurier) 33–4, 36
'reciprocal identity support' (Moss and
    Moss) 25, 29
relationship with deceased partners
    key aspects (Moss and Moss) 24–5
    caring 24–5
    closeness and intimacy 24–5
    commitment and loyalty 24–5,
        101–2
    family feelings 24–5, 123
    interdependence 23–4
    love 23–4
    and self-identity 25
relationship with new partners
    acknowledging differences 37–8,
        84, 90, 95, 106
    and child resentment 56–8
    emotional bonding 52
    introducing to children 60–1
    making changes 34–5, 69, 106,
        108
    questions and self-doubts 43–4,
        52, 83
    and self-identity 29

timing and taboos 28, 67–72,
    76–7, 101
    see also gender differences; sexual
        relationships
religious beliefs
    'Heaven' and afterlife 39, 82, 87,
        92, 94, 109, 132, 139
    mourning rituals 18–21, 74, 85,
        86, 109–10, 119
remarriage
    religious observances 19–21
    social acceptability 32, 75, 81
    see also relationship with new
        partners; three-way
        relationships
resentment feelings 57–8, 113, 125,
    130–1
Richard's story 85–8, 100–2
rings *see* wedding rings
rituals and grief 17–21, 28, 74, 80, 85,
    86, 109–10, 119, 131–2
    importance 18
    religious observances 18–21

school assemblies 18, 80
'seeing' deceased persons 29, 54, 76,
    80–1, 127–8
self-esteem 29
self-identity 29
    loss through bereavement 25, 48,
        99
    and new partners 29
    re-emergence 98
    as 'victim of loss' 43
self-knowledge through grief 22
sexual relationships 44–5
    and ageing 44–5, 104
    comparisons with previous
        relationship 43, 76
    and emotional closeness 47

female perspective 50–2, 89
male perspective 47–8, 100–1
and number of previous
    relationships 44, 89
timescales 45–6, 101
Shiva 19–20, 85
silence 27
Simon's story 80–2
'sit Shiva' 19–20, 85
social events, invitations 51–2, 125
'soulmates' 112–15, 136
stages of grief (Kübler-Ross) 16–17,
    68–70
sudden death 105–7, 137–8
    and suicide 102–4
suicidal feelings 73
suicide 102–4
    following bereavement 46
    partner reactions 21, 102–4
    and taboos 104
Survivors of Bereavement by Suicide
    (SOBS) 148
Suzie's story 132–3

taboos 70–2
    about 'moving on' 28, 67–72,
        76–7, 97, 101
    about suicide 104
    'speaking ill of the dead' 84
tears 15
three-way relationships 31–42
    new partner's perspective 33–4,
        36–8, 39–41, 126–32
    widowed person's perspective
        28–9, 32–3, 120–6
    see also relationship with new
        partners
Tony's story 107–9
The Tortured Mind of Grief and Love
    39–42

uninvited opinions 69–70, 82
    see also judgements and opinions

visualising deceased person 29, 54, 76,
    80–1, 127–8

War Widows' Association of Great
    Britain 149
WAY Foundation 88–9, 91, 93, 96, 149
wedding rings 77, 84, 96, 113, 135
Winston's Wish 57, 88, 149
women and bereavement
    feeling judged 70–1, 91, 134–5
    grieving process 99, 136–7
    life expectancy 50
    motherhood 50–1, 74, 121
    relationship 'opportunities' 51, 89,
        136
    and sexuality 50–2
    as 'threats' 51–2

Author index

Branther, J. 142

Du Maurier, D. 33–4, 36
Dunn, M. 19, 50

Emerson, S. 29–30

Freud, S. 16, 142

Gibran K. 70, 72
Goldberg, H. 48

Halpin, B. 47–8

Jennings, E. 72

Kübler-Ross, E. 15–17

Monaghan, L. 142
Moss, M.S. and Moss, S.Z. 24–5

Neruda, P. 22

Philomen 22

Rilke, R.M. 141

Scott Holland, H. 29–30
Shakespeare, W. 55–6, 142
Staudacher, C. 46